Access to Justice in Environmental Matters

Access to Justice in Environmental Matters

A Socio-Economic Analysis

Michael Faure & Niels Philipsen (Eds)

METRO

Published, sold and distributed by Eleven International Publishing
P.O. Box 85576
2508 CG The Hague
The Netherlands
Tel.: +31 70 33 070 33
Fax: +31 70 33 070 30
e-mail: sales@budh.nl
www.elevenpub.com

Sold and distributed in USA and Canada
International Specialized Book Services
920 NE 58th Avenue, Suite 300
Portland, OR 97213-3786, USA
Tel: 1-800-944-6190 (toll-free)
Fax: +1-503-280-8832
orders@isbs.com
www.isbs.com
Eleven International Publishing is an imprint of Boom uitgevers Den Haag.

ISBN 978-94-6236-075-4
ISBN 978-94-6094-816-9 (E-book)

Printed in The Netherlands

Table of Contents

List of Abbreviations

ADR	Alternative Dispute Resolution
AIR	All Indian Reporter
CJEU	Court of Justice of the European Union
COM	European Commission
EAP	Environment Action Programme
ECHR	European Convention of Human Rights
ECJ	European Court of Justice
ECtHR	European Court of Human Rights
EIA	Environmental Impact Assessment
EU	European Union
IPPC	Integrated Pollution Prevention and Control
MS	Member States
NGO	Non-Governmental Organisation
PIL	Public Interest Litigation
SAL	Social Action Litigation
SCC	Supreme Court Cases (Supreme Court of India)
TEU	Treaty on the European Union
UNECE	United Nations Economic Commission for Europe

1 Introduction

Michael Faure and Niels Philipsen

1.1 Background for This Book

The basis for what is generally referred to as access to justice is constituted by Article 9 of the Aarhus Convention, which provides (if particular conditions are met) access to information, public participation in decision-making and access to justice in environmental matters. In that sense it is generally held that the Aarhus Convention has three pillars. EU law has to a large extent dealt with the first two pillars: access to information and public participation. In 2003 two directives were made that largely dealt with these two pillars: the Access to Information Directive (2003/4/EC) and the Public Participation Directive (2003/35/EC). In the same year a third proposal was introduced (COM(2003)624), directed at implementing the provisions related to the third pillar (access to justice). That proposal, however, led to strong opposition in some Member States, as a result of which the Commission did not pursue the promulgation of that draft directive.

1.2 Recent Developments

There are a few recent developments that have put the issue of access to justice in environmental matters in the EU and hence the implementation of the third pillar of the Aarhus Convention back on the agenda. One particular issue is that the entry into force of the Lisbon Treaty is important since it formally enshrines a right to legal protection of rights and it also incorporates the Charter of Fundamental Rights. Article 19(1) of the Treaty on European Union (TEU) includes an explicit reference to sufficient remedies to ensure effective legal protection. Article 47 of the Charter on Fundamental Rights also covers the conditions of access, including legal aid.

A second and equally important development is that there have been cases by the (then) European Court of Justice (ECJ) dealing with access to justice in environmental matters. In 2008 the ECJ decided the *Janecek* case (C-237/07), where the court recognised a citizen's entitlement to challenge the absence of an air quality management plan despite German law considering that the citizen had no standing to bring such a case. In a subsequent decision of 2011 concerning the *Slovak brown bear* (C-240/09), the court found that Article 9(3) of the Aarhus Convention had no direct effect, but the Member States courts nevertheless had to facilitate access by environmental NGOs.

The scope of 'Directive 2003/35/EC in respect to the drawing up of certain plans and programmes relating to the environment' is relatively limited, as it focuses only on installations falling under the Integrated Pollution Prevention and Control (IPPC) Directive and on cases where an Environmental Impact Assessment (EIA) is required. One question that arises after the *Slovak brown bear* case is whether environmental NGOs should also receive access to justice in environmental matters in cases that do not fall under the EIA or IPPC Directives.
These recent developments hence show that at least the European Court of Justice attaches great importance to Article 9(3) of the Aarhus Convention, apparently also in areas not covered by the IPPC and EIA Directives.

1.3 VARIOUS OPTIONS

The sketch of recent developments (1.2) makes clear that following the more recent case law the European Commission felt urged to take some action in the area of access to justice in environmental matters. However, it is less clear in what direction this action should go. Theoretically, four different options could be examined in this respect:

1. Business-as-usual (soft-law approach). This would involve the existing cooperation with judges and stakeholders and perhaps some guidelines explaining the significance and implications of EU law, but no major changes;
2. Addressing any existing gaps in Member State provisions for ensuring access to justice on the basis of Article 258 TFEU. This would obviously imply that Member States would implement the consequences of the *Janecek* and *Slovak brown bear* cases. It would imply that the Commission would use its enforcement powers to make sure that the consequences of the case law are also implemented by Member States;
3. Drafting a new legislative proposal (or significantly amend COM(2003) 624) targeted more precisely on entitlement to access implied by the cases *Janecek* and *Slovak brown bear*,[1] with the conditions of access mirroring those already established for EIA. The difference with option 2 would be that in this case the consequences of the new developments (sketched in 1.2) would also be incorporated in a new directive;
4. Sticking to the original proposal, *i.e.* COM(2003) 624, with possible minor modifications.

The goal of this book is to examine the advantages and disadvantages of the four options that were just sketched to push forward access to justice in environmental matters in the EU.

1 Relevant case law, including *Janecek* and *Slovak brown bear*, is discussed in Chapter 2 of this book.

1.4 Methodology

This book will pursue, as the title makes clear, a socio-economic analysis of access to justice. This implies that the first methodology that will be followed consists of Law and Economics, also referred to as the economic analysis of law. Attention will be paid to the potential costs and benefits of the various options just sketched (1.3) using economic tools. Obviously, a pure cost-benefit analysis in the traditional sense may not be possible. However, a key feature of the Law and Economics methodology is that it pays ample attention to the way in which various legal rules affect the behaviour and incentives of stakeholders. Hence, an economic analysis of procedural law will be used to indicate how a variety of legal rules (more particularly with respect to access to justice) affect the incentives of stakeholders in a trial.

The economic approach followed here does not merely involve a so-called rational choice analysis, assuming that all parties involved in the trial are rational utility-maximising actors. Nowadays, increasing attention is paid to the so-called behavioural approach where psychological notions are used to explain how parties may behave in reality. Finally, an important argument at the EU level is undoubtedly that differences in access to justice may endanger the level playing field in the EU which would necessitate a harmonising intervention. Hence, this argument of the level playing field will also be examined. These three economic approaches (rational choice, behavioural approach, and levelling the playing field) will be sketched in general, but more importantly, their implications for access to justice will be sketched.

Hence, to some extent this book goes beyond the narrow topic of access to justice in environmental matters. To an important extent, a broader Law and Economics analysis of access to justice will be provided whereby these general insights will next be applied to the specific case of access to justice in environmental matters and more particularly the four options for further action at EU level.

In addition to an economic analysis, this book will also pursue a Law and Society approach. Public Interest Litigation (PIL) has in many developing countries had a strong influence and the results of the arguments advanced in that literature in favour of increased access to justice and PIL will be presented and critically discussed. Again, the relevance of those arguments for the access to justice in environmental matters in the EU will be critically assessed as well.

Finally, in addition to these theoretical approaches, an empirical study will be conducted. This consists of a survey whereby access to justice in environmental cases in particular Member States will be examined, mostly from the perspective whether the different options that we just presented (in 1.3) would lead to particular consequences in the countries under examination. Obviously, this will not be a full empirical investigation of access to justice in environmental matters in all Member States. A few Member States (more particularly Latvia, the United Kingdom and Germany) were selected. The reasons for selecting those countries were (as will be explained in Chapter 6) that they had striking differences as far as access to justice in environmental matters is concerned.

1.5 LIMITS OF THIS BOOK

This book focuses, as was just mentioned (see 1.4), on a socio-economic approach to access to justice in environmental matters. The goal of our book is not to examine to what extent Member States accurately implemented the environmental acquis with respect to access to justice, nor the Aarhus Convention. One of the reasons we do not focus in this book on the legal perspective on access to justice in environmental matters is that a lot of information is already available on the status quo in this respect in the Member States.[2] Therefore, our focus is on the socio-economic aspects of access to justice in environmental matters, a topic which, to our knowledge, has not been the subject of an in-depth study yet. However, we do not aim to provide an impact assessment of the costs of access to justice. Indeed, as we explained, we provide an analysis of access to justice in environmental matters from various methodologies (sketched in 1.4), but we do not aim at providing a regulatory impact assessment, nor a cost-benefit analysis, since the data and tools for such an analysis are simply lacking. Instead, the four options of access to justice are examined from a Law and Economics and Law and Society perspective.

1.6 STRUCTURE

Chapters 2 and 3 of this book provide the legal background and a closer examination of the four options, respectively. Chapter 4 provides the economic framework for analyzing access to justice in environmental matters, both from a theoretical perspective and applied to the four options. The results of our Law & Society analysis are presented in Chapter 5. Chapter 6 contains a small number of country studies. The empirical analysis contained in that chapter, in which the results obtained in the theoretical study are tested by means of interviews, is crucial since it provides indications on how stakeholders experience the differences between the four options. Conclusions and policy recommendations are presented in Chapter 7.

2 For this legal perspective, see a 2012 report for the European Commission coordinated by Prof. Jan Darpö, available at: <http://ec.europa.eu/environment/aarhus/pdf/2012_access_justice_report.pdf>.

1.7 Contributors

The contributors to this book are all affiliated with the Faculty of Law of Maastricht University, based in the Netherlands. The book is the result of a collaboration between environmental lawyers (Chris Backes), specialists in civil procedure (Fokke Fernhout), Law and Economics scholars (Michael Faure, Manuela Mühl and Niels Philipsen) and Law and Society scholars (Leïla Choukroune).

Originally, the research which constituted the basis for this book was carried out by the Maastricht European Institute for Transnational Legal Research (METRO) at Maastricht University. The original study is available online.[3] However, the contributors to this book have worked further on the text. The current book hence consists of an improved version of the report which was originally drafted for the European Commission.

1.8 Acknowledgements

As editors, we are grateful to the many people who made this book possible. We are especially grateful to the contributors for their willingness to participate in this highly challenging and interesting project, working under strict deadlines imposed upon them.
We especially owe thanks to the Environment Directorate-General of the European Commission and more particularly to Adam-Daniel Nagy, Liam-Joseph Cashman and Jean-François Brakeland for a very stimulating and pleasant collaboration and for useful and stimulating feedback on earlier drafts of the report that constituted the basis for this book. We equally owe thanks to the administrative centre of the Maastricht European Institute for Transnational Legal Research (METRO) and especially to the METRO support office for editorial assistance in the preparation of this book for publication. Finally, we are most grateful to our publisher Eleven international publishing for their kind and efficient support in the publication of this book.

The texts were finalised in May 2013, and for that reason, developments after that date have not been taken into account.

3 At <http://ec.europa.eu/environment/aarhus/pdf/access%20to%20justice%20-%20economic%20implications%20-%20study%202013.pdf>.

2 Legal Background

Chris Backes, Michael Faure and Fokke Fernhout

The legal situation concerning access to justice in environmental matters in 17 EU Member States has recently been studied by a research team coordinated by Prof. Jan Darpö.[1] For that reason, as we mentioned in the introduction, we are not going to focus on the legal analysis of access to justice in environmental matters in EU Member States. However, in order to make a socio-economic assessment of the different options for further action at EU level, it is of course important to provide briefly the status quo in the EU in this respect. This is precisely the goal of this chapter, whereby we will focus on the Aarhus Convention (2.1), current EU law and proposals (2.2-2.3) and the case law of the ECJ (2.4). Section 2.5 provides the summary.

2.1 The Aarhus Convention

Starting point for access to justice is Article 9 of the 'Aarhus Convention on access to information, public participation in decision-making and access to justice in environmental matters'. The "third pillar" of the Aarhus Convention calls for a reasonable entitlement to access (also referred to as *locus standi*) and reasonable conditions of access (*i.e.* fair and effective procedures in terms of time and costs). Article 9(2) of the Aarhus Convention provides that

> [e]ach party shall, within the framework of its national legislation, ensure that members of the public concerned
>
> (a) Having a sufficient interest
>
> or, alternatively
>
> (b) Maintaining impairment of a right, where the administrative procedural law of a party requires this as a precondition,

1 Study on the implementation of Arts 9.3 and 9.4 of the Aarhus Convention in 17 of the Member States of the European Union, carried out by Jan Darpö and others, see: <http://ec.europa.eu/environment/aarhus/pdf/2012_access_justice_report.pdf>.

> have access to a review procedure before a court of law and/or another independent and impartial body established by law to challenge the substantive and procedural legality of any decision, act or omission subject to the provisions of Article 6.

What constitutes a sufficient interest and impairment of a right shall be determined in accordance with the requirements of national law.
Article 9(4) of the Aarhus Convention provides that the procedures referred to in paragraphs 1, 2 and 3 "shall provide adequate and effective remedies, including injunctive relief as appropriate, and be fair, equitable, timely and not prohibitively expensive".
Article 9(3) of the Aarhus Convention provides that in addition parties must also ensure that,

> where they meet the criteria, if any, laid down in its national law, members of the public have access to administrative or judicial procedures to challenge acts and omissions by private persons and public authorities which contravene provisions of its national law relating to the environment.

In sum, Article 9(2) concerns review procedures relating to projects falling under Article 6, while Article 9(3) concerns review procedures for review of acts and omissions of private persons or public authorities contravening provisions in national environmental law. Related to both, Article 9(4) provides minimum standards applicable to access to justice procedures, decisions and remedies.[2]

2.2 DIRECTIVE 2003/35/EC

Some of these obligations under the Aarhus Convention have also been transposed in EU law. Two directives from 2003 implement the two first pillars of the Aarhus Convention in EU law.[3] Most important for the purposes of this study is Directive 2003/35/EC, which provides for public participation in respect to the drawing up of certain plans and programmes by amending the EIA Directive and the IPPC Directive.[4] The preamble to Directive 2003/35/EC explicitly refers to Articles 9(2) and (4) of the Aarhus Convention. The goal of this Directive is to guarantee access to justice in two distinct areas of environmental law: cases where an EIA is necessary, as regulated by Council Directive 85/337 of

---

2 Stec & Casey-Lefkowitz 2000, p. 125.

3 2003/4/EC (Access to Information Directive) and 2003/35/EC (Public Participation Directive). Regulation 1367/2006 covers the implementation with regard to the EU Institutions.

4 *OJ* L156/17 of 25.6.2003.

27 June 1985,[5] and cases related to IPPC, as regulated by Directive 96/61.[6] The scope of the Directive 2003/35 is hence relatively limited. The Directive only provides a legal framework for access to justice in Member States if it concerns decision-making with respect to IPPC installations or if an EIA is required.[7]

2.3 Proposal COM(2003) 624

Almost at the same time as the promulgation of Directive 2003/35/EC with its limited application to EIA and IPPC, a proposal was launched to provide a broader access to justice. Indeed, Directive 2003/35 only intended to implement Articles 9(2) and (4) in relation to the provisions of Article 6 of the Aarhus Convention.[8] However, Article 9(3) of the Aarhus Convention refers to broader possibilities whereby Member States are obliged to provide members of the public access to "administrative or judicial procedures to challenge acts and omissions by private persons and public authorities which contravene provisions of national law relating to the environment". The Commission proposal on access to justice in environmental matters, COM(2003) 624 of 24 October 2003, precisely had as its goal to provide this broader access to justice in environmental proceedings for members of the public and for qualified entities (see Article 1 of the proposal). The latter was considered by some Member State experts as going beyond Article 9(3) of the Aarhus Convention.[9] Interestingly, this proposal mentions that additional costs following from the implementation of the proposal could be limited. The following arguments were provided:

- All Member States already have in their constitutional systems, judicial and administrative structure to ensure the correct application of their legal systems. Since these structures as such already exist in the Member States, additional costs on that issue are not expected.
- However, the recognition of environmental NGOs foreseen by the proposal may place some administrative burden on Member States, which may lead to some additional costs.
- Minor additional costs may also be incurred by the judiciary owing to a potential increase of legal proceedings in environmental matters.
- Based on past experience, this increase of proceedings in environmental matters will be small in relation to the total number of legal proceedings.
- The additional caseload can be handled within the framework of existing judicial systems.

---

5 *OJ* L175 of 5.7.1985, amended by Directive 97/11/EC, *OJ* L73, of 14.3.1997 and now revised and superseded by Directive 2011/92/EU, *OJ* L26, of 13.12.2011.

6 *OJ* L257, of 10.10.1996, now Directive 2008/1/EC, *OJ* L24 of 15.1.2008.

7 See Jans & Vedder (2012), p. 232.

8 This is *inter alia* made clear in consideration (9) preceding Directive 2003/35, which explicitly refers to Art 9(2) and (4) of the Aarhus Convention.

9 COM(2003) 624 final, p. 8.

- Competent public authorities will have to do a preliminary review, which may lead to some additional expenses, but this would also imply that no heavier burden would be placed on the judiciary.[10]

The proposal also mentions substantial expected benefits from the new instrument such as:
- Greater compliance by operators and public authorities with environmental provisions in order to avert enforcement orders that would create additional costs for them.
- Related to this: preventive effects, leading to lower expenditures for public authorities in the field of environmental protection.
- A better distribution of the economic burden of repairing and compensating for environmental damage among taxpayers.
- Reduction of social costs since enforcement of environmental law will lead to less environmental damage to be compensated *ex post*.[11]

Notwithstanding these alleged advantages of the proposal (limited costs and potentially huge benefits), the Commission apparently had difficulties convincing the Member States. Already during the consultation rounds preceding the 2003 proposal, many Member States raised substantial concerns (related to, *inter alia*, the requirement to provide standing to groups without legal personality, giving standing on the basis of pre-defined criteria for qualified entities, and administrative requirements),[12] and the opposition from some Member States was apparently so strong that legal doctrine holds that the proposal can, politically speaking, be considered "dead".[13]
There are, however, reasons to put the idea of an EU-wide directive on access to justice in environmental matters again on the political agenda. One can, in this respect, refer to the entry into force of the Lisbon Treaty,[14] but also to the potential cost of inaction.[15] These costs of policy inactions, also with respect to access to justice, have recently again been highlighted in an academic study.[16] In addition, one can point at the different reports from the Commission on implementing community environmental law, where not only the problem of the implementation deficit is stressed, but also the importance of access to justice as a tool of enforcing European environmental law.[17] In a recent Communication on

10 COM(2003) 624 final, p. 7.
11 COM(2003) 624 final, p. 8.
12 COM(2003) 624 final, pp. 8-9.
13 Jans & Vedder 2012, p. 236.
14 See in this respect also Pallemaerts 2009.
15 Already referred to in the proposal COM(2003) 624 final, p. 5.
16 Bakkes *et al.* 2008.
17 See *e.g.* the communication implementing community environmental law from 22 October 1996 COM(96) 500 final, especially pp. 11-13.

implementing European Community environmental law, the Commission stresses again with respect to the earlier proposal (COM(2003) 624) that:

> The Commission remains of the view that community environmental law would be better and more consistently enforced if the proposed Directive were adopted. Making it easier to bring cases before a national judge should enable problems to be resolved closer to the citizen. It should also reduce the need for Commission intervention.[18]

There have also been some recent developments regarding the political context that are worth mentioning in this respect. The European Parliament and the Council have already taken initial positions concerning the mentioned proposal. In the "European Parliament resolution of 20 April 2012 on the review of the sixth Environment Action Programme and the setting of priorities for the seventh Environment Action Programme" it is underlined that the seventh EAP should provide for the full implementation of the Aarhus Convention, in particular regarding access to justice. The European Parliament stressed in this connection the need to adopt the proposed Directive on Access to Justice and calls on the Council to respect its obligations resulting from the Aarhus Convention and to adopt a common position on the corresponding Commission proposal before the end of 2012.[19] In addition, the Council conclusions on the seventh EAP also called for the improvement of access to justice in line with the Aarhus Convention.[20] Moreover, in the context of the European Parliament Report on a collective redress working paper, the European Parliament has called upon an EU instrument on injunctive relief in the environmental field.[21]

This shows that recently (Spring 2012) there has been increased political pressure (at least from the European Parliament) to adopt the proposed Directive on Access to Justice and to fully implement the Aarhus Convention. However, probably the most important reason to put access to justice in environmental matters back on the policy agenda is recent developments in ECJ case law.

---

18 COM(2008) 773 final, p. 6.

19 European Parliament Resolution of 20 April 2012 on the review of the sixth Environment Action Programme and the setting of priorities for the seventh Environment Action Programme – A better environment for a better life (2011/2194 (INI), 68).

20 See the conclusions on setting the framework for a seventh EU Environment Action Programme at the 3173rd ENVIRONMENT Council Meeting (Luxemburg, 11 June 2012): – improving complaint handling at national level, including options for dispute resolution, such as mediation; – improving access to justice in line with the Aarhus Convention.

21 European Parliament Resolution of 2 February 2012, "Towards a Coherent European Approach to Collective Redress" (2011/2089 (INI)). Here the European Parliament takes the view that the need to improve injunctive relief remedies is particularly great in the environmental sector, while calling on the Commission to explore ways of extending relief to that sector.

2.4 Case Law

There have been a number of evolutions in case law with respect to access to justice. Without addressing these to the full extent within this project that mainly focuses on economic analysis, it can be held that they clearly demonstrate an "activist" approach to access to justice in environmental matters by the ECJ.[22] Some of these evolutions in case law are of such an importance that they seem to imply that Member State action in the area of access to justice in environmental matters will be necessary, even if Member States would remain reluctant to accept proposal COM(2003) 624 enlarging access to justice beyond Directive 2003/35/EC (awarding access to justice only with respect to cases falling under the EIA and IPPC Directives). A few recent cases can illustrate this:

Although normally a principle of procedural autonomy of Member States law is accepted, the *Janecek* case seems to put some limits to this procedural autonomy.[23] The Court held that Article 7(3) of Directive 96/62 of 27 September 1996 on ambient air quality assessment and management (Air Quality Framework Directive) must be interpreted as meaning that, where there is a risk that the limit values or alert thresholds may be exceeded, persons directly concerned must be in a position to require the competent national authorities to draw up an action plan. The importance of the decision is that the Court of Justice applies a wider interpretation of the concept of an "impairment of a right" than is common in German law.[24] Different from the *Trianel* case (see hereafter), in the *Janecek* case the widening of the scope of applicants who can claim a right derived from EU environmental law to get access to court concerned individuals.

An even more recent case C115/09 (*Trianel*) of 12 May 2011 confirms this line of reasoning. German law limited the right to challenge decisions to cases where individual rights would be violated. The Court decided that a consequence of Directive 2003/35/EC, inserting Article 10a and especially subsection 3 thereof in the Directive 85/337, is that it precludes legislation

> which does not permit non-governmental organisations promoting environmental protection [...] to challenge before the courts, in the context of an action contesting a decision authorizing projects "likely to have significant effects on the environment" [as defined in the amended EIA Directive], the infringement of a rule flowing from EU environment law and intended to protect the environment, on the ground that that rule protects only the interests of the general public and not the interests of individuals.

22 Jans & Vedder 2012, p. 231. See also the country reports from the Darpö study.

23 Case C-237/07 *Janacek* (2008) ECR I-6221 of 25 July 2008.

24 Jans & Vedder 2012, p. 231. It should be noted, however, that the ECJ decision is directly based on Art 7(3) of the amended Directive 96/62 and does not give an interpretation of what would amount to an impairment of a right or which interest should be sufficient to be granted standing.

In other words, the court held that NGOs promoting environmental protection can have access to justice even where (on the ground that the rules relied on protect only the interest of the general public) national procedural law does not permit this to individuals.[25] The so-called *Djurgården* case (which is also related to Directive 2003/35/EC) dealt with a reference for a preliminary ruling from a court in Sweden on public participation in environmental decision-making procedures.[26] In this particular case, a local Swedish NGO had appealed a decision concerning the construction of a tunnel. The appeal by the NGO was held to be inadmissible because it had not fulfilled the conditions laid down in the Swedish Environmental Act, stating that it must have at least 2,000 members. The ECJ argued that members of the public concerned

> must be able to have access to a review procedure to challenge the decision by which a body attached to a court of law of a Member State has given a ruling on a request for development consent, regardless of the role they might have played in the examination of that request by taking part in the procedure before that body and by expressing their views.

The Court equally held that Article 10a of the amended EIA Directive

> precludes a provision of national law which reserves the right to bring an appeal against the decision on projects which fall within the scope of that directive, as amended, solely to environmental protection associations which have at least 2,000 members,

since that would impair the essence of the objectives of Directive 85/337 (para. 47). Legal doctrine holds that this decision not only has serious consequences for Swedish procedural environmental law, but also for the law of other Member States, *e.g.* the Netherlands.[27] Finally, the *Slovak brown bear* case (C-240/09 of 8 March 2011) must be mentioned here, which did not deal with Directive 2003/35, but Article 9(3) of the Aarhus Convention. In this rather spectacular case the court had to decide on whether Article 9(3) is directly effective. Answering a reference for a preliminary ruling the ECJ holds the following:

> Article 9(3) of the Convention on access to information, public participation in decision making and access to justice in environmental matters approved on behalf of the European Community by council decision 2005/370/EC of 17 February 2005 does not have direct effects in European Union law.

25 *Trianel* judgement (C-115/09), consideration 59.
26 Case C-263/08 *Djurgården-Lilla Värtans* (2009) ECR I 9967 of 15 October 2009.
27 For details see Jans & Vedder 2012, pp. 232-235.

> It is, however, for the referring court to interpret, to the fullest extent possible, the procedural rules relating to the conditions to be met in order to bring administrative or judicial proceedings in accordance with the objectives of Article 9(3) of that convention and the objective of effective judicial protection of the rights conferred by European Union law, in order to enable environmental protection organisations such as the L.Z., to challenge before a court a decision taken following administrative proceedings liable to be contrary to European Union law.

This means that the ECJ basically holds that the national court has to interpret its national law in accordance with the objectives laid down in Article 9(3) of the Aarhus Convention. Legal doctrine holds that this case can have important consequences for access to justice in environmental matters. Some scholars argue that the consequence is that Article 9(3) of the Aarhus Convention is applicable across the full breadth of European environmental law.[28] This would mean that environmental groups should be allowed access to a court to challenge decisions that might conflict with environmental law of the Union.[29] However, other legal scholars doubt whether this interpretation is correct. The Court explicitly decided that direct application of Article 9(3) is not possible. Therefore, application of this provision will not be possible where national law leaves no room for interpretation. This seems to be the case, *e.g.* in Germany, Austria and some other countries. Other scholars are of the view that a so-called zero option for interpretation is not acceptable. This would mean that if there is no national legal framework for NGO standing, a national judge would still be obliged to give standing based on this court ruling. Hence, it can be seen that there are diverging views, and that the Slovak case judgement may reduce the differences in the application of Article 9(3) of the Aarhus Convention within the Member States, but it may do so only to a certain extent.

2.5 Summary

This brief overview shows that the legal situation as far as access to justice in environmental matters is concerned is, to put it mildly, rather complex. Directive 2003/35/EC and subsequent case law (more particularly the Djurgården and Trianel cases) provide a broad interpretation of possibilities of access to justice if the EIA and IPPC Directives apply. However, the case law demonstrates that the interpretation and application of Article 9(2) of the Aarhus Convention still significantly differs in the Member States.

28 For this interpretation see Ebbeson 2011.

29 So also Jans & Vedder 2012, p. 237.

The most important development probably arrives in the domain of Article 9(3) of the Convention. Whereas EU Member States opposed the proposal COM(2003) 624, which suggested a broader access to justice in environmental matters precisely to implement Article 9(3), such a broader access to justice now seems to be realised to a certain extent along the line of Court of Justice of the European Union (CJEU) case law. After all, the recent Slovak case forces national courts to interpret law as much as possible in such a way as to enable environmental NGOs, in line with Article 9(3) of the Aarhus Convention, to challenge administrative environmental decisions in Member States. However, this will not ensure the full application of Article 9(3) in all Member States, because the space for such an Aarhus-conform interpretation of national law depends on the wording of the national law and the national doctrine of international law conform interpretation of national law. It may be expected that the judgment in the Slovak case will not eliminate substantial differences between EU Member States in the application of Article 9(3).

Moreover, it is likely that in the future more requests for preliminary references will follow, aiming to clarify issues of standing on which there still is uncertainty. Questions could be asked concerning the precise interpretation of the standing and procedural rules, *i.e.* with respect to what should be considered as timely, costly, etc. Currently (Autumn 2012), several cases dealing with Directive 2003/35/EC are pending. Especially the *Edwards* case (C-260/11), the *Krizan* case (C-416/10) and the *Altrip* case (C-72/12) should be mentioned in this respect.

These evolutions, in sum, show that many Member States may anyway be forced to change their national legislation to bring it in line with the obligations resulting from the Aarhus Convention as interpreted by the ECJ. However, some Member States will probably not adjust their law and hence infringements of the Aarhus Convention will remain.

3 Examining the Four Options

Chris Backes, Michael Faure and Fokke Fernhout

The rather turbulent evolution concerning access to justice in environmental matters shows that a variety of options exists that would result in more or less far-reaching harmonisation of access to justice in environmental matters. The goal of this book is to analyse what the precise consequences of the various options would be for the stakeholders involved. The four options will be sketched below, but first attention will be paid to the main differences between the status quo and the intended Directive in proposal COM(2003) 624.

3.1 COM(2003) 624 versus the Status Quo

We will first analyse shortly what the main differences are between the intended directive as shaped in the proposal COM(2003) 624 final (hereafter "the proposal") and the current legal situation, taking into account the recent case law of the CJEU.

Article 3 of the proposal ensures that members of the public, where they meet the criteria laid down in national law, have access to "environmental proceedings" to challenge acts and omissions by private persons that are in breach of environmental law. The declared intention of the proposal with regard to this provision is to not go beyond what is required on the basis of Article 9(3) of the Aarhus Convention. Therefore, discretion remains with the Member States to identify further criteria in national law that have to be met in order to obtain access to justice in such situations. This means that Article 3 presumably cannot be said to be unconditional to be directly applied if a Member State does not transpose this requirement properly or does not apply it adequately. As Article 9(3) of the Aarhus Convention already contains the same requirement and, according to the *Slovak* case, Member States are already obliged to interpret their national law as much as possible, Article 3 of the proposal will bring about no legal changes.

That is different with regard to Article 4 of the proposal. This article transposes the requirement of Article 9(3) to ensure that members of the public have access to justice to challenge the procedural and substantive legality of administrative acts or omissions that may breach environmental law. The prerequisites that national law may require for those seeking access to justice are the same as laid down in Article 9(2) of the Aarhus Convention. As the CJEU case law demonstrates, the discretion of the Member States on this point (Art 4(2) of the proposal) is more limited than the discretion with regard to Article 9(3) and hence does not prevent that this provision would be directly applicable if not correctly transposed into national law. Therefore, Article 4 of the proposal would potentially make a difference. Until now, Directive 2003/35/EC requires Member States to ensure access to justice only in cases falling under the EIA Directive or IPPC Directive. It needs to be examined whether the law of the Member States differentiates between those cases and other cases where environmental law provisions could be infringed. If it does, it further should be examined whether the result that Article 4 of the proposal wants to guarantee differs from what would be possible with an interpretation of the national law in accordance with Article 9(3) of the Aarhus Convention as such a Treaty-conform interpretation of the national law on access to justice of members of the public is required already now.

Article 5 of the proposal concerns legal standing of "qualified entities". The proposal requires access to justice for such entities in all kinds of "environmental proceedings", just as Directive 2003/35/EC requires standing for such entities only in procedures covered by the IPPC or EIA Directive. Hence, the changes that Article 5 of the proposal would bring about depend on the question whether the law of the Member States already provides such an access to court in conformity with Article 9(3) of the Aarhus Convention and, if not, whether the law of such Member States may (and thus must) nevertheless be interpreted in accordance with this requirement. The importance of this provision is that the requirement of sufficient interest or impairment of a right does not hold for these qualified entities when the qualified entity is recognised in accordance with Article 9. This has already been implemented in Directive 2003/35/EC. The question is whether the *Slovak brown bear* case implies that the same line of reasoning should be followed in environmental cases that are not covered by the changes brought about by this directive.

Article 6 of the proposal requires something completely new, compared with the Aarhus Convention. Member States have to ensure that someone who has legal standing according to Articles 4 and 5 must have access to an objection procedure within the administration. The competent administrative authority has to decide within 12 weeks on such an objection. There is no provision in the Aarhus Convention requiring such an objection procedure. Therefore, this would add a new element to what is required already now, even if a far majority of EU Member States already have such a procedure.

Another new element is the procedure to recognise entities that have the objective to protect the environment and the criteria for recognition of such qualified entities (Arts 8 and 9 of the proposal). Some Member States already know such procedures, and others do not. The Aarhus Convention does not require a recognition procedure, but the introduction thereof is understandable in relation to the extensive standing that is granted to these qualified entities under Article 5.

To sum up, the main differences the proposal would bring about compared with the current legal situation are the requirement of an objection procedure and the introduction of a procedure to recognise entities that aim to protect the environment (Arts 6, 8 and 9 of the proposal), together with an unimpaired legal standing for recognised qualified entities.

Articles 3, 4 and 5 transpose (possibly partly) existing requirements of Article 9(3) of the Aarhus Convention. However, these requirements may not have been transposed or may not be applied in all Member States. If the law of a Member State is deficient, it has to be interpreted as much as possible in accordance with Article 9(3) of the Aarhus Convention. If the room for such an interpretation is too limited to meet all requirements of Article 9(3), the proposed directive may change the legal setting, as its provisions can directly be applied and as this direct application can be enforced at the courts of the Member States. This is true with regard to Articles 4 and 5 of the proposal, but not with regard to Article 3, as this article is not sufficiently unconditional.
Having said that, we now may compare the effects of the four options introduced above.

3.2 Option 1: Business as Usual (Soft Law Approach)

The first option is only to rely on existing cooperation with judges and stakeholders and to rely on a form of commentary or guidelines explaining the significance and implications of Treaty provisions and case law. This would hence mean that one would work towards the implementation of the Aarhus Convention but not take substantial further action.
The disadvantage of this approach, at first blush, may be that it is difficult to predict in what direction evolutions will go. Therefore it may also be difficult for stakeholders to assess costs. Indeed, Section 2.4 sketched some evolutions in case law, but as long as Member States have not taken action, this can result in substantial uncertainty, which in itself can be costly. An objection procedure would not be introduced in the countries where this is not yet required. The same holds with regard to the procedure for the recognition of entities that aim to protect the environment. Existing gaps in the transposition and application of Article 9(3) of the Arhus Convention would remain to a large extent.
In addition, above we already referred to the costs of non-implementation of the *acquis communautaire*. These costs of inaction would hence remain. Also, the infringement cases are of course case-based and it may take a long time before all Member State laws are brought in accordance with EU law as interpreted by the ECJ.[1]

3.3 Option 2: Addressing Existing Gaps in Member States Provisions

The second option is for the Commission to use Article 258 TFEU to address existing gaps in Member States law to ensure access to justice. This would basically mean that

1 In this respect we refer to the total *social* costs. Since the increased access to justice would remedy externalities, these total social costs would be reduced. However, for one individual Member State implementation can still lead to costs.

recent case law, more particularly the *Trianel*, *Janecek* and *Slovak* cases, would be used to force Member States to comply with EU law. With regard to the objection procedure and the procedure for recognition of entities, this option would, like option 1, bring about no change. This option can only partly guarantee the full implementation and enforcement of the requirements of Article 9(3) of the Aarhus Convention. Therefore, differences in the application of existing (international) law would be diminished to a certain extent, but would also remain to a substantial extent. A level playing field cannot fully be realised. A difficulty with this approach is, as with option 1, that one would not only have to refer to the current CJEU case law, but also speculate on the outcome of a few pending infringement cases, as for example, the case referred by the *Bundesverwaltungsgericht* on 12 January 2012 (C-72/12).
In addition, this approach may have the disadvantage that some uncertainty remains, while a full level playing field is not created. In those respects, option 2 would amount to similar problems found under option 1.

3.4 Option 3: Drafting a New Proposal

A third proposal would be to withdraw[2] or significantly amend COM(2003) 624, which was, as mentioned, opposed by many Member States. A new legislative proposal would *inter alia*:

- Implement entitlements to access as implied by the ECJ case law discussed above in Section 2.4;
- Mirror access to justice according to the access already awarded under the public participation directive (2003/35/EC);
- Could basically implement emerging case law to formulate relevant provisions.

The difference with COM(2003) 624 is that it probably would not aim at going beyond the scope of the Aarhus Convention regarding access to justice as in the original proposal and that it would not require the Member States to introduce separate administrative procedures (Art 6 of the proposal and probably also Arts 8 and 9 of the proposal). There seems to be also a general consideration of aiming to bring the text closer to the already existing access to justice provisions of the Directive 2003/35/EC. The advantage would be that:

- All CJEU case law on the Aarhus Convention would be applicable and requirements as regards Article 9(3) would be implemented;
- The opposition against COM(2003) 624 final could (perhaps) be tackled;

2 Withdrawal means in this context that a new Directive would be also proposed in parallel, with substantial modifications from the withdrawn text.

- By incorporating case law into the directive, one would basically force Member States to do what they anyway have to do;
- Codifying the case law would create more clarity on its content and meaning; and
- The approach would (contrary to options 1 and 2) create more legal certainty for operators in Member States, not create new costs for new procedures, reduce the costs of inaction and hence also create a level playing field for industry.

3.5 OPTION 4: RETAIN COM(2003) 624

This would basically mean that the existing proposal would be retained with only minor modifications and to try to provide new (also economic) arguments to gain political support.

The advantage may be (like in option 3) that costs of inaction are reduced and that, to a certain extent, a level playing field is created. However, the introduction of new procedures (Arts 6, 8 and 9) may cause additional costs. A disadvantage is perhaps that it may still be difficult to gain political support, given the strong opposition that existed in 2003. It should, however, be noted again that the circumstances have changed, due to the recent case law, but also due to the fact that many countries have joined the EU since 2003.

The goal of the project as far as this aspect of the research is concerned is to sketch more precisely what the effects of the four options would be for the stakeholders involved (operators, judiciary, NGOs, administrative authorities) in terms of awarding more or less access (entitlement) and the corresponding conditions. The goal of the project is of course not normatively to formulate a preference for one of the four options. However, it may be possible, at the end of the project, to indicate a preference for one or more of the options after a more careful economic and empirical analysis.

4 Incentives, Costs and Benefits: A Law and Economics Analysis

Michael Faure, Manuela Mühl and Niels Philipsen

In this chapter we will present an economic analysis of the effects of an increased access to justice. First, we will introduce some basic economic principles of litigation (4.1), including the notion that verdicts are considered as 'public goods'. The theoretical framework that follows in Section 4.2 focuses on a *'social welfare' approach*, where the role of the judiciary, the law, the jurisdiction and the litigation process come to the fore, in relation to the goal of maximising social welfare. Next, the theoretical framework reflects on a so-called *behavioural approach* by explaining the incentives of judges and other stakeholders in the litigation process (4.3). The behavior of potential plaintiffs and defendants will be analysed in more detail by distinguishing between the different stages of a litigation process: precaution, suit, settlement and trial. A more applied study of the economic arguments concerning legal standing in environmental matters finishes this section (4.3.7).

In Section 4.4 we will address the four options central to this study in more detail, by applying the economic insights to each of the four scenarios defined in Chapter 3 of this report. Next, we will discuss the question to what extent "levelling the playing field" could be an important consideration and argument in favor of a more harmonised approach (4.5). We conclude this chapter by formulating a number of hypotheses, based on the economic analysis (4.6). These hypotheses will be tested in the empirical part of this study.

As an indication for the reader, it should be stressed that the first three sections of this chapter (4.1-4.3) are rather technical, discussing the economic literature in a fairly detailed manner. The insights from those sections are subsequently used to discuss the four options (4.4) and the question to what extent levelling the playing field for industry and for the citizens[1] in Europe is of importance (4.5). The reason for this set-up is that the theoretical Sections 4.1-4.3 provide the basis for the further economic analysis of the four options (4.4) and the issues related to levelling the playing field (4.5). Reading Sections 4.1-4.3 is not necessarily required for an understanding of Sections 4.4 and 4.5. Hence, the reader who wishes to have a quick access to the most important issues of relevance for this study may turn directly to Section 4.4, where the theoretical insights presented first are applied to the four options.

1 The way in which the level playing field argument is usually addressed in the literature is by referring to the incentives of industry to relocate. That is also the approach that we take in this report. One could equally examine whether there is a level playing field for plaintiffs, *e.g.* standing for NGOs. To some extent that is simply the mirror image of the level playing field for industry.

It should be noted at the beginning of this chapter that the economic analysis of dispute resolution strongly relies on the hypothesis of one party suffering a loss (a victim) who brings a claim against another party as defendant who presumably caused the loss (the injurer). That is a model of litigation different from the typical cases of access to justice in environmental matters, which usually concern cases before administrative courts. In those cases the defendant is not a 'traditional polluter' as envisaged in the economic literature on litigation, but an administrative authority deciding, *e.g.* on an environmental impact assessment or the granting of a permit to an IPPC installation. These authorities are primarily supposed to act in the public interest, protecting citizens and the environment, and not only take into consideration the interests of industry (who would be a traditional defendant in an adversary litigation case). Although we do realise that the model in administrative cases related to access to justice in environmental matters, covered by the Aarhus Convention, is often fundamentally different from that discussed in the economic literature on litigation, we believe that to an important extent this literature still remains relevant. After all, even when an administrative authority in an Aarhus-type administrative procedure is not directly comparable to a defendant in private litigation, formally the administrative authority is a defendant to whom a plaintiff addresses a claim, *e.g.* for injunctive relief (Art 9(4) of the Aarhus Convention). Moreover, Article 9(3) addresses access to administrative or judicial procedures to challenge acts and omissions by private persons and public authorities which contravene provisions of national law relating to the environment. Hence, the economic analysis that follows in Sections 4.1-4.3 is directly applicable to situations of judicial procedures where members of the public challenge acts or omissions by private persons. That is a traditional plaintiff-defendant situation as viewed by the economic analysis of civil procedure. Moreover, by way of a practical example, in the UK, challenging acts of public authorities can only be done by means of judicial review, which means that the rules of civil procedure (and hence the litigation model of the following paragraphs) fully apply.

In administrative law cases, the situation is of course slightly different, but from the perspective of the members of the public, the public authority in an administrative procedure will position itself as a defendant even though the procedure is structured in a different manner.

4.1 An Introduction to the Economic Analysis of Litigation

4.1.1 *Verdicts as Public Goods*

The production of justice has particular positive side-effects, which go beyond the interests of the parties involved in a legal dispute. Third parties who are not directly involved in the conflict may learn from the outcome and avoid similar conflicts and costs. The use of the information embodied in a verdict is non-rivalrous and the exclusion of future litigants from that information is undesirable. Court decisions can therefore be categorised as 'public goods'.[2] These characteristics make dispute resolution particularly well-suited for production by states, because states are best capable of capturing its 'external' benefits. Indeed, all EU Member States provide court services at subsidised prices. This implies that the social net benefits of dispute resolution resolved by public courts are expected to exceed the costs of subsidies. The renowned professor Steven Shavell once stated that "litigation will be worthwhile to society as long as its deterrent and compensatory value exceeds total legal costs plus public administrative expenses".[3] This very basic finding is of course relevant in an Aarhus-context as well: when administrative courts decide, *e.g.* that a member of the public can be awarded injunctive relief, this provides social benefits which can be qualified as positive externalities. Not only will the environment benefit from such a decision (which is the goal of the Aarhus Convention, but can be considered as an economic benefit as well); the decision also provides information to third parties, which equally can be considered as a positive externality.

4.1.2 The Demand for Trials

The total amount of litigation is determined by the number of conflicts which, in turn, depends on many factors. The determinants of legal conflicts include, *inter alia*, the level of care taken by potential plaintiffs and defendants, legal costs (and how these are allocated among the parties), quality of law and precedents, time investment for the dispute resolution, prosperity of the economy and people's customs.[4] Whether conflicts between parties actually reach the courts depends on the decisions taken by each of the parties concerned in each stage of the litigation process. Moreover, any determinant of the decision-making in the post-conflict phase (*e.g.* the costs of legal procedures) impacts not only on decisions taken in the subsequent stages of the dispute, but also on decisions taken earlier, such as the decision on how much precaution to take in the pre-conflict phase. By estimating the costs of the 'worst-case scenario' of a trial, individuals determine their optimal level of precaution *ex ante* by investing in precautionary measures.[5]

For both (potential) plaintiffs and defendants it can be argued that the demand for trials is mainly determined by legal costs, the way they are allocated and the perceived chances of winning a case.[6] More specifically, with regard to the Aarhus Convention, a member of the

2 Samuelson 1954. According to economic theory, public goods are defined by two criteria: non-rivalry and non-excludability.

3 Shavell 1982a, p. 71.

4 Mühl & Vereeck 2003.

5 Posner 2010.

6 *Ibid.*

public seeking access to justice will balance his private costs[7] versus the benefits of obtaining, *e.g.* injunctive relief prohibiting an environmentally damaging activity in his neighbourhood. The balancing exercise for the defendant may be different, depending upon whether the defendant is a private person (*e.g.* industry) or a public authority. Whereas private defendants will balance private costs and benefits, public authorities[8] should also have the public interest in mind.

4.1.3 *Individual Decision-Making and Welfare*

Taking a social welfare approach, the aim of litigation is to minimise the total costs of legal disputes for society. Of course, it is impossible to calculate the benefits and costs of legal disputes precisely. The value of a verdict cannot be determined since there is no functioning market for verdicts. It is possible, however, to estimate whether effects are positive or negative and to draw welfare-economic conclusions on this basis.[9] From a welfare-theoretical point of view the costs of prevention (*i.e.* precaution) and the costs of legal conflicts have to be balanced. The aim is to find the optimal level of precaution, which can only be reached if the costs and benefits of a trial, including the probability of winning or losing a case, can be estimated correctly.

As we mentioned before (see Section 4.1.1) decisions in Aarhus-type cases can be considered as public goods or positive externalities. On the one hand these decisions can promote environmental quality and thus reduce the negative externality caused by environmental harm. On the other hand they can create positive externalities to third parties benefiting from the information generated through the decision-making process. More specifically, these third parties may learn from the outcome of the case and avoid similar conflicts and costs in the future.

4.2 Access to Justice: A Social Welfare Approach

4.2.1 *The Judicial System*

The law and order of states is divided in different institutions with restricted competences. This separation of powers has the purpose to define the rights of individuals in an economy

7 This does include not only his costs of legal representation and the actual costs of going to trial, but also the so-called opportunity costs (time spent on the trial in which no other beneficial activities can be undertaken).

8 A public authority can balance, in the public interest, the costs and benefits of a particular decision and, within the court setting, of resisting against the plaintiff's claim or not.

9 See also Cooter & Rubinfeld 1989, pp. 1067-1097, referring in this context to Kaldor-Hicks efficiency (which in essence boils down to a cost-benefit analysis).

(legislative), to provide an authorised system to solve legal disputes (jurisdiction), and to take care of the prosecution of illegal action (executive).[10] The efficiency of a judicial system depends on all elements of the legislation, jurisdiction and the execution of the jurisdiction. These elements should aim at the maximisation of welfare, and can theoretically be assessed by a cost-benefit analysis.[11] Inefficiencies of the judicial system lead to a loss of welfare.[12] A judicial system that is not capable of deterring damaging or illegal actions, or includes the production of legal mistakes, creates costs for society. The loss of positive externalities that are borne in a legal verdict, the creation of legal uncertainty and a loss of faith in the judicial system can all increase future costs of legal conflicts and therefore have to be included into the estimation of the efficiency of a legal system.

Schwartz and Tullock have defined three categories of costs that occur as a result of an unlawful action for society: costs of the illegal action itself, costs of pursuit and sentencing, and costs of judicial mistakes due to sanctioning the innocent or not (sufficiently) sanctioning the guilty.[13] Determining the social costs of the judicial system, either theoretically or empirically, is very complex.[14] The problem lies in the fact that the output (*e.g.* justice, environmental protection) cannot easily be measured or quantified. This also holds for the preferences of the individuals concerning public goods.[15]

Compared with out-of-court settlements, the sum of private and public expenses are always higher if a conflict comes before court. This is the reason why economists generally prefer settlements over trials.[16] Trials only lead to a reduction in social costs if they generate positive externalities, if they lead to improvement of law, or if the private benefits of a verdict go beyond a strict re-distribution.[17] Below we will provide a more detailed economic analysis of the trade-off between legal procedures on the one hand and settlements (including alternatives like mediation) on the other.[18]

4.2.2 *The Contribution of Law*

4.2.2.1 Providing Legal Certainty

According to Law and Economics literature, laws should create *legal certainty*. Individuals must be able to correctly estimate the degree of right and wrong of their actions. This is

10 Schwartz & Tullock 1975.
11 *Ibid.*; Posner 1973.
12 Tullock 1980.
13 These are the so-called type I-and type II-errors, respectively. Schwartz & Tullock 1975; Becker 1968. See also Section 4.2.3.1.
14 Cooter & Ulen 2011, p. 386.
15 Olson 1973.
16 Shavell 1999.
17 Shavell 1982b; Gravelle 1990.
18 See Section 4.3.4.

important in order to reach an optimal level of investment in precaution. If there is full legal certainty, one would expect a socially optimal number of legal suits. Only in the case of unclear legal rules or following socio-economic changes, an increase in the number of suits and trials would occur. This dynamic process of adaptation of law would then again result in legal certainty.

Inefficiencies appear if the law is not able to avoid repeated trials on the same or similar subject matter. This is the case when the law is not clear for these cases, or if there is room for strategic use of the courts. The costs that arise to society as a result of these repeated trials could have been avoided and are, thus, "unnecessary costs". The law should then be re-formulated as to improve legal certainty and avoid strategic moves by parties.
A high level of trials is not per se inefficient. However, a distinction must be made between the various reasons for trials. Opportunistic trials are always inefficient, since the aim of the trial is not to administer justice and hence there is no social benefit of this trial. This is different for other types of trials. For example, in a changing society and economy, the law has to undergo certain adaptations, which can be realised by trials and their verdicts. If legal uncertainty arises due to these changes in society, trials are socially desirable and external benefits of suing can be captured. Selective suits will lead to more efficient law in the future, since unclear laws will be more often the reason for trials and will be interpreted over and over by judges until they become "good" laws.[19] It should be noted though that private incentives to sue and social goals often do not fully align. The parties to a legal dispute are not (always) taking the social benefit of their dispute into account and may hence exclude it from their decision-making.
Although this reasoning is based on the economic perspective on private litigation, it is highly relevant for Aarhus-type litigation as well: as we mentioned above (see 4.1.1) Aarhus-type litigation can create high social benefits in terms of promoting environmental quality (remedying negative externalities), creating public goods and positive externalities. However, given the private costs of litigation (see 4.1.2) an undersupply of Aarhus litigation may occur. This again justifies the question whether lower cost alternatives (like settlements or mediation) should be promoted.[20] Aarhus litigation can reveal information to members of the public and public authorities and hence contribute to legal certainty. The analysis presented here makes clear that legal certainty is important also from an economic perspective, to the extent that it plays a role in remedying market failures (such as externalities and undersupply of public goods). Below we will, when examining the four options in more detail, stress that from an economic perspective the extent to which the options create legal certainty for the stakeholders involved will be a crucial criterion.

19 Cooter & Rubinfeld 1990.
20 See Section 4.3.4.

4.2.2.2 Disclosure of Information

In a first step after a suit, procedural common law prescribes the way in which information relevant to the case will be disclosed. In civil law, the opposing parties will exchange views and arguments in a pre-lawsuit debate. By this, opponents and their lawyers are able to estimate the legal position and the consequences of a suit or trial. This aims at a correction of possible wrongful estimations and hence to (more) legal certainty in this matter.[21] If the estimations about the value of the claim/verdict and the chance to prevail in court of both parties are correct (*i.e.* the law is clear) an out-of-court settlement can probably be reached, because the parties base their estimations on a correct and just basis.[22] If the available information about the correct value of a legal claim is not sufficient, although the law as such is clear, the defendant is not able to choose an optimal level of precaution in advance of a legal claim, nor is he able to decide on a correct settlement offer after suit. In this case a trial becomes likely. A too low level of precaution and a trial are socially undesirable, because the law as such is clear.[23]

Research on the efficiency of procedural law is not conclusive about obligated disclosure of information. The disclosure of information in the stage of trial leads to administrative and transaction costs, which could be avoided by an out-of-court negotiation.[24] Transaction costs resulting from legally obligated disclosure, in particular related to information exchange and negotiations, are to be borne by the parties themselves. This means that the costs are taken into account in the calculation of private costs. Since this procedure is under legal obligation, these costs always arise, even if the case is not going before court (*e.g.* because the parties have settled before the beginning of a trial).[25] In the most favourable case, the direct costs for using the public courts can be avoided.[26]

Judges as well as the parties can request an external expert when they need more information. The selected expenditure level for the acquisition of these experts is justified from a social perspective if the costs do not exceed the benefits of finding the truth on the basis of the new information, *i.e.* if the expenditure lowers "error costs". Following Shavell it is not possible, however, to theoretically determine whether the expenditures from a social point of view will be excessive or too small.[27] The legislator reserves the right to intervene in case of allegedly excessive private expenditures of the parties by, *e.g.* limiting the number of the experts or witnesses, and/or determining time restrictions.

---

21 See Cooter & Ulen 2011, pp. 391-399.
22 Shavell 1997.
23 Cooter & Ulen 2011.
24 Allen 2000; Cooter & Ulen 2011.
25 Cooter & Ulen 2011.
26 Posner 1973, p. 400.
27 Shavell 1997, p. 610.

Now that the importance of disclosing information and the role of the legal procedure in this disclosure process has been stressed from an economic perspective, we can again link this to the Aarhus Convention. Interestingly, the Convention in Article 9(5) recognises the importance of disclosure of information by mentioning explicitly the duty for the signatory states to disseminate information to the members of the public on access to justice rules. This obligation to disseminate such information fits perfectly into the economic logic presented above, considering the trial also as a device of information disclosure. It also follows on the economic benefits of Aarhus litigation, repeatedly mentioned above (see Sections 4.1.1 and 4.1.3). Given these identified economic benefits of Aarhus litigation the duty to disclose information to the public on access to justice contained in Article 9(5) makes economic sense.

4.2.3 The Jurisdiction

In the following, economic analysis will be applied to determine the efficiency of jurisdiction. It is necessary in this respect to consider different elements: the efficiency of single proceedings, the possibility of suits for cases with a trifling nature of the offence, and cost-shifting rules concerning the direct costs of litigation.[28] Jurisdiction should aim to efficiently punish illegal action. In other words, it must optimise the compensation of the victim and the execution of the laws, in order to reach the goal of minimising the number of conflicts and thus cost-intensive trials to society.[29]

According to Posner, the social costs of a trial can be separated into direct and indirect costs.[30] Direct costs include costs of the lawyers, judges, and time invested. Indirect costs arise from the failure of the juridical system to achieve allocative and other goals.[31] Furthermore, when addressing social costs it is useful to make a distinction between private and public costs. The private costs of a legal conflict are the sum of all pre-conflict costs for precautionary expenditures, transaction costs (including lawyer costs), court fees, and opportunity costs. The public costs of a legal conflict result from the costs of judges, buildings, personnel, equipment, etc. Moreover, external costs may arise, *e.g.* due to wrong decisions being made by judges. Those are referred to as *error costs*, to be discussed below.

The objective of the public jurisdiction should be to minimise the sum of the total social costs, *i.e.* the sum of the private, public and external costs of legal conflicts and to maximise the benefit of trials due to their positive externalities.

---

28 Posner 1973, p. 401.
29 Tullock 1980; Shavell 1997.
30 Posner 2010, p. 400.
31 Posner 1973. See also Cooter & Ulen 2011, pp. 384-386.

Two categories of errors in judgments can be differentiated: type I and type II-errors. A type I-error refers to the condemnation of an innocent person. A type II-error refers to a situation where the guilty are set free, or where guilt can be correctly determined, but the judgement is inadequately soft.[32] In the context of administrative law, a type I-error would mean punishing an applicant for bringing an environmental protection case before the court. Type II errors in this context would mean that harm is caused to the environment if the inadequate administrative measure is not appropriately controlled by the judge, as an administrative judge not only potentially punishes, but also has a role of controlling administrative decision-making. Both error types will reduce the efficiency of the jurisdiction and represent thereby a source for social costs.[33] An efficient court system requires a jurisdiction where unlawful action will be discovered correctly and sanctioned appropriately.[34] The beneficiaries of an accurate jurisdiction are those members of society that are able to avoid a suit and trial (positive externalities of trials), and only in second line the parties that meet before court. The generation of positive externalities therefore justifies that public courts are subsidised, as we already indicated in the beginning of this chapter.

By having to interpret the law repeatedly, judges are able to improve the law. The aim must be to optimise the demand for trials, by balancing the costs and benefits of the jurisdiction. Excessive subsidisation of courts would stimulate inefficient or even unauthorised complaints before court (*moral hazard*), since it might offer advantages to a large number of plaintiffs and its lawyers to bring a suit. From a social welfare perspective, public means should be used particularly to improve the correctness of the jurisdiction, because thereby direct as well as indirect costs can be lowered on a long-term basis by the creation of legal certainty. It should become clear that the direct and indirect costs are interdependent.[35]

Tullock discusses law itself as a source of error. The more detailed the law, the clearer the judicial situation and the interpretation of legal conflicts.[36] However, this is only possible up to a certain degree. Too many details also lead to complexity, which can become a source of conflicts, or they lead to a restricted applicability.[37] As a consequence, the number of laws would increase. The more complicated the law, the higher the expenditure and time investment for its interpretation. The costs of new legal rules are not only restricted to the costs of formulation and publication, but also include additional search costs in order to determine the degree of guilt or innocence. As soon as there is a possibility for interpretation given, the parties will be inclined to invest more in the interpretation of the

32 See Cooter & Rubinfeld 1990 and Posner 1973. These judgmental errors are often named alpha and beta errors.
33 Posner 1973, p. 401.
34 Tullock 1980; Gravelle 1995.
35 Posner 1973, p. 441; Posner 2010.
36 Tullock 1980; Tullock 1994.
37 Tullock 1980, p. 178.

law to their favour. This is likely to increase social costs, without generating (m)any social benefits.[38]

At this moment it is important to recall that from an economic perspective one of the goals to be achieved during the trial is a reduction of error costs. In other words, in the Aarhus-context, the identified benefits of litigation (see Sections 4.1.1 and 4.1.3) should preferably be achieved at lowest error costs. Precisely in order to reduce those costs, procedural guarantees, involvement of lawyers, etc. have often been mandated, which in turn create administrative costs. The balance between on the one hand administrative costs (aimed at the reduction of error costs) and on the other hand the error costs themselves will be crucial, for example in the trade-off between litigation and its alternatives (like mediation).[39]

4.2.4 Costs of Litigation

The legislator and judges can take measures to reach the social goals of the jurisdiction. In this section we consider both desired and unwanted effects of such measures.

In the economic literature, theoretical models have been presented that estimate the total social costs and benefits of the judicial system. Posner, for example, has argued that total social costs consist of the sum of social costs and error costs of trials.[40] The social costs result from the sum of both parties' private costs for the case and the public costs for the maintenance and supply of the court apparatus, in other words, the sum of direct private and public costs.[41] Shavell has estimated the private costs of a trial as being lower than the public costs. The private benefit of a judicial conflict resolution results from the compensation of the plaintiff for damage suffered, which actually has a purely redistributive character. The social benefit of trials results from the positive externalities of jurisdiction.[42] The sum of the external, public and private costs, minus the positive externalities (*e.g.* deterrence of illegitimate actions) and private benefits is called the total social loss.[43] The term 'loss' implies that the total social costs exceed the total social benefit. This model is based on the fact that cases are expensive and that they also cause social costs in addition to the private costs borne by parties to the dispute. The aim should be to make the parties 'internalise' the social (*i.e.* external) costs of the conflict resolution process, including the costs that arose to third parties.[44]

38 *Ibid*, p. 184.
39 See on this point also Section 4.3.4.2.
40 Posner 2010.
41 Shavell 1982b.
42 *Ibid.*, p. 333.
43 Becker 1968; Shavell 1982b; Cooter & Rubinfeld 1990.
44 Cooter & Rubinfeld 1989; p. 1069 and p. 1090; Posner 1973.

It is undoubtedly necessary that courts function well by making correct judgements. All societal entities, *i.e.* individuals and firms, must be able to rely on the courts to estimate just or unlawful action and to be (as much as possible) certain that unlawful action experienced by them will indeed be prosecuted and sanctioned. Access to justice and correctness in judgments are the core aims of an efficient court system. This requires also a relatively low cost of using the courts.[45]

These observations constitute in a way a summary of the economic approach to litigation as presented above. Litigation, also in Aarhus-cases, creates costs and benefits. Shavell's point is that private benefits may be lower than social benefits. In the Aarhus-context this could arise, *e.g.* because a litigant only views his personal benefit of getting injunctive relief which he seeks in an administrative procedure. However, social benefits (in terms of improved environmental quality, creating public goods, or information generation) can be substantially higher. That underscores Tullock's point that society has an interest in stimulating access to justice, given the positive benefits generated by litigation. This reasoning hence provides the basic economic motivation why it could be in society's interest to stimulate access to justice.

The other point stressed by Tullock relates to the fact that litigation can also result in wrong decisions, leading to error costs. In order to minimise those the marginal administrative costs of, *e.g.* investing in representation and procedures (in order to increase quality) should be weighed against the benefits in reduction of error costs.

4.3 Access to Justice: A Behavioural Approach

4.3.1 *Incentives of the Judiciary*

Before now analysing the incentives of various stakeholders in the judicial process, we will focus on probably the most important stakeholder, being the judiciary itself. There is an important literature explaining the incentives of judges. This literature may at first sight seem rather exotic and strange to the legal community, but it has the advantage that it may shed some light on the welfare functions of judges and the corresponding attitudes one can expect from judges when caseloads would increase, *e.g.* due to a widened access to justice. Especially since this literature is also of an empirical character,[46] it may be interesting to briefly summarise this literature at this point.

Economic literature basically holds that judges, like everybody else, are rational utility maximisers. This issue has been stressed for example by Cooter (1983) and Posner (1993). Both authors assume that judges dislike effort.[47] Cooter assumes that judges providing

45 Tullock 1980; Posner 1973; Posner 2010.

46 Although most of it is US-based.

47 Beenstock & Haitovsky 2004, p. 352.

private services have a financial incentive to increase their caseload (and hence their income). In Posner's approach, focusing on federal judges, income is fixed and can hence not be increased by more efforts.[48] He defines judicial utility as a function of income, leisure and judicial voting.[49] Since income of federal judges is fixed, maximising leisure becomes especially important, in addition to other components of utility such as popularity, prestige and reputation.[50] Judges therefore balance leisure and judging without endangering other components of the utility function, like reputation.[51] Posner further predicts that especially judges who have reached a high income level (*e.g.* Supreme Court Justices) will prefer to maximise leisure.[52] Furthermore, "the opportunities for a leisured judicial life, especially at the appellate level, are abundant".[53] Hence one can especially at Supreme Court level expect measures by judges to reduce their workload.

In theory, judges confronted with an increased workload could maximise leisure by simply deciding fewer cases. This would unavoidably lead to increased court congestion and a backlog of cases. This could harm the reputation of judges and will hence be avoided.[54] Judges could also lobby the legislator for more judges to deal with increasing workloads. However, this would reduce the prestige of the judges and evidence shows that judges to the contrary would rather work harder under pressure in order to avoid congestion.[55] The judiciary may thus look for alternative ways to reduce their workload.

There is some empirical evidence supporting Posner's hypothesis that judges maximise their utility.[56] Helland and Klick recently showed that judges in class action cases have an incentive to easily grant the attorney's fee request in order to terminate cases rapidly, thus avoiding court congestion (which may damage their reputation).[57] Research from Israel also shows that judges, for reputational reasons, will avoid a large backlog and hence dispose of more cases when the caseload increases.[58] Other research shows that a higher workload increases the probability of retirement of judges.[59]

---

48 Posner's approach builds further on his work with Landes on the independence of the judiciary (see Landes & Posner 1975).

49 Posner 1993, p. 2.

50 *Ibid.*, pp. 13-15 and Stras 2006, p. 1430.

51 The importance of maximising leisure for judges was recently repeated by Posner in his book *How Judges Think*. See Posner 2008, p. 77.

52 In his words: "I therefore predict that a higher judicial salary is likely to reduce the amount of work done by existing judges". See Posner 1993, p. 33.

53 Posner 2008, p. 61.

54 Helland & Klick 2007, p. 173; Beenstock & Haitovsky 2004, p. 353.

55 Beenstock & Haitovsky 2004, p. 368.

56 See *inter alia* Stras 2006, p. 1419.

57 Helland & Click 2007, pp. 171-173.

58 Beenstock & Haitovsky 2004, pp. 352-353.

59 Nixon & Haskin 2000, pp. 471-472; Spriggs & Wahlbeck 1995, p. 590; Barrow & Zuk 1990, p. 469. For a summary of this literature see Stras 2006, pp. 1436-1437.

This literature on the incentives of the judiciary may also be relevant in the context of the access to justice as guaranteed by the Aarhus Convention. On the one hand, the behaviour of judges in Aarhus-cases may not necessarily be different than in other cases. On the other hand, there is one important (and perhaps slightly worrisome) lesson from this behavioural literature. It does indeed indicate that judges with a fixed appointment may only have incentives to increase their reputation or otherwise to increase leisure by reducing their workload. Given the empirical evidence just presented, it can be expected (without doing any normative assessment on the role of the judiciary) that when increased access to justice leads to an increased workload for the judiciary, this will decrease their leisure time and hence may not be welcomed. *Ceteris paribus* (for example, given a fixed income level), one can hence expect a utility-maximising judge to interpret Aarhus litigation in such a way that access to justice will be limited. The simple reason is that increased access to justice increases their workload which, given the theoretical and empirical evidence, may be disliked by the judiciary. If one wishes to draw normative conclusions from this finding it may be an argument in favour of alternative solutions like environmental mediation,[60] assuming that mediators (also depending of course upon their incentive system) may have better incentives to award access to justice in environmental matters than the judiciary. One very important nuance should of course be added: the evidence shows that judges do not only want to maximise leisure, but also reputation. Especially "green" justices with a strong pro-environment motivation may thus be inclined to enlarge access to justice, even if this would increase their workload.

4.3.2 Stakeholder Incentives

In our economic analysis, we focus on the expected costs and benefits of (an enhanced) access to justice for the various stakeholders involved, being the judiciary (courts), administrations, business and potential plaintiffs (NGOs and citizens). Of course, the important observation that litigation helps to solve a prevailing market failure and thereby generates social benefits[61] (in addition to private benefits for NGOs and citizens), including legal certainty, will also be taken into account in the evaluation.

For the stakeholder analysis, we propose a strong focus on *incentive* effects of an increased access to justice, based on the existing literature in the field of procedural Law and Economics, as discussed in the previous section and in the following sections.[62]

60 Which will be further discussed in Section 4.3.4.2.

61 See Section 4.1.

62 Kathryn Spier 2007, in a chapter for the *Handbook of Law and Economics*, provides an excellent overview of this literature.

Regarding a legal conflict in a chronological order four phases can be recognised:[63]

1. the pre-suit phase, where precautionary measures can be taken to avoid a legal conflict;
2. the phase where a damaged party decides to bring a suit;
3. the phase of out of court negotiations; and finally
4. the phase of a trial.

Before and during the conflict, the parties concerned have to make a number of decisions. These decisions by private parties are based on individual trade-offs of costs and benefits. Traditional models on the decision-making process in the different phases have been formulated by Posner and Shavell, respectively.[64] In these models, both parties involved in a legal matter take the worst case scenario for their decision-making into account, *i.e.* a court trial. They, respectively their lawyer, try to estimate the costs and benefits from a trial, which determines their position for pre-trial settlement negotiation. This behaviour underlies the utility-maximisation theory under uncertainty by Raiffa.[65] In general it can be stated that the expected costs and benefits of a trial are the determinants for a particular demand for trials. The more disadvantageous the estimation of a trial, the more precautionary measures will be taken by a potential violator to avoid a legal claim in the first place. This includes the private costs of trial (including *e.g.* direct time investment in the case, loss of orders for an enterprise, or the expected sanction for the potential defendant), and the estimation of the benefits of a trial, determined by the chance to succeed in court.
The number of legal claims rises, if the number of conflict-triggering activities increases, the costs of bringing suit decreases, and the value of the expected court verdict increases. However, one can expect an increasing level of precaution concerning the latter point by potential defendants as to avoid the high compensation payments after a trial.[66]

4.3.3 *Precaution and Conflict Event*

At the beginning of each legal conflict stands a triggering action. The frequency of conflicts depends on the number of activities (for example, the production level), and, in addition, on the precautionary measures taken in order to avoid possible conflicts caused by those actions. Precautionary measures are often expensive, *e.g.* the costs of filtering installations for industrial production or the negotiation of certain non-standard contract-clauses.

63 Mühl 2001.
64 Posner 1973, Shavell 1982a.
65 Raiffa 1968.
66 Cooter & Ulen 2011, p. 382 *et seq.*

Economic literature that analyses decisions by individuals in the pre-conflict and conflict-event phase provides us with theoretical models based on behavioural theory.[67] All individuals take into account the expected costs of a possible conflict when they decide on their optimal degree of precautionary measures. The costs of expensive legal proceedings will be balanced against the costs of precaution.[68] A 'rational' decision would minimise the sum of precaution costs and net costs of a trial, where the latter factor is discounted by the probability of a trial. This probability is influenced by the level of precaution, because the higher the level of precaution, the lower this probability will be. In general, for most individuals the expected costs of a trial (*i.e.* the last phase in a legal dispute) are likely to be higher than the benefits.[69] This leads to incentives by both parties to a conflict to invest in precaution.
The individual decisions regarding the prevention level might be inefficient from a social welfare perspective.[70] As discussed before, legislators have different measures at their disposal. By applying liability rules it is possible for the legislator to give incentives to private parties to take an optimal level of precautionary measures. This means that even when contracts between parties are not possible, an internalisation of costs to private parties in the form of damages can – theoretically – be guaranteed.[71] The effect of liability is simple: unlawful action will be sanctioned and this influences the net costs of a trial.[72]

4.3.3.1 Enforcement of a Legal Claim

A party suffering damage broadly has two options. The damage can be demanded directly, without assistance from a third party. The compensation will then be negotiated between the damaged party (victim) and the causer (injurer). The so-called 'transaction costs' of the dispute would be relatively low in this case. However, the party suffering damage can also decide to contact a legal expert or the court, which involves much higher transaction costs. In practice an intermediate form of both solutions may occur, where direct negotiations between victims and injurers in an early stage of the dispute are followed by support provided by lawyers in order to put emphasis on the claim when negotiations seem to lead to an undesired result.
According to the Law and Economics literature, a rational person will sue for compensation if the costs of suing and maybe trial do not exceed the expected benefits.[73] The expected private benefit consists of the compensation that is expected by the claimant. The higher the value of the claim, the lower the costs of negotiations and legal steps are, and

67 See *e.g.* Van Velthoven & Van Wijck 1997; Cooter & Ulen 2011; Cooter & Rubinfeld 1989.
68 Van Velthoven & Van Wijck 1997.
69 *Ibid.*
70 Shavell 1999.
71 See also Cooter & Rubinfeld 1989, p. 1085.
72 *Ibid.*, p. 535.
73 Shavell 1982b; Posner 2010; Cooter & Rubinfeld 1990.

the more optimistic the damaged party is regarding the probability of success in a trial. The costs for the claimant include transaction costs, time, direct costs of the lawyer and the court, costs of obligated procedures, experts, and other expenses.[74]

In economic theory it is often assumed that a damaged party considers claiming damage compensation against a causer only if he has a credible threat. This requires that the private costs of claiming do not exceed the compensation by the (expected) verdict.[75] Following this argumentation it is realistic to assume that a damaged party will not bring a suit in case of a non-credible threat although the law is clear and in his favour. Even if he would do so, the causer has no motivation to compensate for the damage, knowing that further judicial steps are disadvantageous to the claiming party. In such situation damage will continue because the judicial system fails.[76]

In case a damaged party has a credible threat, the causer will balance the costs and benefits of an out-of-court settlement and a court trial.[77] It is possible, though, that a claiming party did not suffer damage at all. The reasons for such situations lie in asymmetrical information between the parties or strategic behaviour on the part of the claimant, which possibly create purely monetary advantages or other advantages like damaging the reputation of an opponent. The possibility that it could end in a trial and hence lead to higher costs compared to a settlement may put pressure on the potential defendant.[78]

The reasoning above shows, as we explained in the introduction to this chapter,[79] that the economic reasoning developed from a private litigation perspective. However, as we indicated already, the reasoning applies also to the Aarhus-context. A plaintiff in an 'Aarhus-suit', for example, seeking injunctive relief against a permit that was according to him wrongly granted, will (either implicitly or explicitly) engage in a cost-benefit analysis that will determine his incentives to sue. Also for the Aarhus-claimant the crucial element will be whether he has a credible threat against the defendant (either a private person or a public authority in the sense of Article 9(3) of the Aarhus Convention) and will indeed balance the costs of settlement versus litigation.[80] Let us now briefly address the different cost elements that may affect the plaintiff's incentive to start legal action.

4.3.3.2 Costs of Bringing a Legal Claim

Assuming rational behaviour, whether or not a party brings a suit depends (among other factors) on the expected costs of a trial. Court fees therefore have a direct influence on

74 Cooter & Ulen 2011, pp. 382-418; Cooter & Rubinfeld 1989, 1990.

75 Van Velthoven & Van Wijck 1997; Menell 1983.

76 Menell 1983; Van Velthoven & Van Wijck 1997, p. 211 *et seq.*

77 *Ibid.*

78 Bebchuk 1988; P'ng 1983.

79 See Section 4.2.

80 This balancing between settlement and litigation, including alternatives such as mediation, will be further discussed in the next section.

the number of suits. Also, the effect of a higher burden of proof for the victim, unfavourable liability rules or lower compensation payments after a trial have the same effect as an increase of the court fee for legal dispute resolution.[81] An increase in the costs of a suit and/or a decrease in the net benefit of a trial will diminish the number of credible threats. The limit of the claim for damages will increase compared with the situation with a lower court fee (if we ignore strategic considerations). The legislator can influence the number of credible threats by a change in the legal compensation payment. Awarding a higher compensation, the expected benefit of a complaint increases and this will result in a higher number of credible threats.[82]

The grant of a pro deo lawyer is meant to make it possible for financially disabled parties suffering damage to bring a suit, independent of the costs of legal dispute resolution. This also gives incentives to potential causers to also take complaints by poor parties seriously, thereby internalising the external costs of damage to these poor parties. The possibility of having a pro deo legal advisor hence can turn a previously non-credible threat into a credible threat, which is likely to generate social benefits.[83]

Again, here we can refer to the reasoning that from an economic perspective (Aarhus) litigation can have benefits and that for that reason litigation should in these cases be stimulated.[84] Extensive economic literature exists concerning the question how barriers to access to justice can be reduced. Much of this literature is focused on private litigation, for example on empowerment of victims in environmental matters and on victims of personal injury cases[85] but the basic point applies to Aarhus litigation as well: if there are social benefits resulting from this litigation, measures supporting litigants in bringing claims should be economically justified.

The basic problem in environmental matters is no different from the basic problem in the consumer area: social benefits of litigation may be large, but the private incentives may be limited, for example, because private benefits for one plaintiff can be rather small. This creates the divergence between the private and social incentives to sue, identified by Shavell.[86] That means that from an economic perspective there will often be an undersupply of litigation in environmental cases, for example because of the widespread nature of the damage. The result is that the individual loss for each victim is very small which leads to the phenomenon of "rational apathy": given the very low individual benefits victims of environmental harm become "apathic" and rationally disinterested. However, from society's perspective, litigation is then undersupplied. This provides arguments both for

81 *Ibid.*
82 Cooter & Rubinfeld 1989.
83 Van Velthoven & Van Wijck 1997, p. 237 *et seq.*
84 See the summary in Section 4.2.4.
85 See the contributions in Tuil & Visscher 2010.
86 Discussed above in Section 4.2.4.

facilitating access to justice to environmental NGOs as well as for remedying risk aversion of potential litigants (aversion more particularly against high costs of litigation) and collective redress.[87] The measures remedying risk aversion include legal aid, as discussed in this subsection, and lowering the barriers to litigation: the widespread nature of the damage could give rise to the necessity of collective redress.[88] Both constitute remedies which are necessary in order for the litigant to constitute a credible threat against the defendant (either a private person or public authority in the sense of Article 9(3) of the Aarhus Convention).

4.3.3.3 Information Asymmetries

The net-expected benefit of a suit and trial in fact is an estimation made by the party suffering damage. That party will have to consider a realistic compensation for the damages suffered, weighed by the probability to win in court, and also the expected costs of a trial. Hence, information (also about the other party) is of great importance, because it determines the expected value of the claim and the chance to prevail in court. Because it is rather unrealistic to assume that private parties and their lawyers have perfect information about every determining factor within a legal conflict, the estimations of the concerned parties to prevail in court and the value of the verdict will differ, *i.e.* there is information asymmetry. If the damaged party is optimistic, he will sue and will be willing to go further to court. The legislator can influence the degree of information by publishing verdicts on compensation payments, interpretations of laws, or prejudices. By this, the number of suits can be influenced indirectly.

4.3.3.4 Collective Redress

Particularly in the United States victims of legal violations have the possibility to bring suit for small damages where the estimated value of a trial does not exceed the costs.[89] The problem of not being able to make use of the social benefits of a claim of trifling nature can be solved by collective redress. Here, the compensation damages are combined into a total complaint sum that exceeds the costs of a trial.

There can be different ways of organising collective redress. In the consumer sphere this often takes the form of a so-called class action. There are many economic arguments

87 Class actions and collective redress are private law concepts, whereas in the context of this research we discuss the corresponding public law concept of access to justice by NGOs. However, many of the economic arguments in favour of collective redress also apply to the case of access to justice for NGOs in the public law context.

88 To be discussed in Section 4.3.3.4.

89 See also Section 4.3.7.

favouring class actions (or more generally collective redress); arguments which apply to environmental litigation as well. Proponents of collective redress point out the positive effects of compensation of damaged victims and sanctioning of illegitimate action. An important justification for collective redress is that the causer of the damage is confronted with the external costs of his or her acting. This is related to the so-called 'allocative responsibility' of the legislature.[90] Further, collective redress creates economies of scale, since costs can be distributed among all members of the class action group. It can therefore be expected that the number of complaints and trials will increase.[91]

Here lies also the argument of the critics of collective redress, because an increased workload obviously creates costs and may lead to problems with respect to the functioning of the courts. It can however be objected to these complaints that the social benefits generated by collective redress justify a higher workload of courts.[92] Bernstein did empirical research on these opposite arguments and found that collective redress in general goes along with several problems. One problem is the absence of plaintiffs and their widespread opinions concerning the case. Bernstein could not find evidence of a significant increase in workload of the courts and concluded that class actions are efficient, maybe even more efficient than conventional trials, and should be promoted from an economic as well as from a moral perspective.

As mentioned, these arguments in favour of a form of collective redress also apply to access to justice in environmental matters and hence to Aarhus litigation. In consumer cases the argument for collective redress is that some harm may be dispersed (scattered losses). Also in relation to environmental harm this will often be the case, except when a nuisance is caused only to a limited number of individuals. Like in the consumer area the same justification for collective redress can be provided in the context of access to justice in environmental matters: since individual environmental harm may be small, private incentives for victims (of pollution) can be very limited as a result of which a suit will not be brought. The benefits of (Aarhus)litigation[93] would then not be realised, resulting in a social loss. This provides a strong argument for collective redress also in environmental cases, especially in case of a widespread nature of the harm. One way of providing this collective redress is precisely Public Interest Litigation (PIL), to be discussed in Chapter 5. We have shown that PIL also has very clear economic foundations: providing a remedy for the widespread nature of environmental damage which would otherwise no longer lead to private incentives to bring Aarhus litigation.

---

90 Posner 2010.

91 See further on collective redress Keske, Renda & Van den Bergh 2010.

92 Bernstein 1978, p. 350.

93 As *inter alia* identified in Sections 4.1.1 and 4.1.3.

4.3.4 *Settlement*

4.3.4.1 General Economic Theory of Settlements

Authors agree that only a small part of legal disputes ends up in trial. Mainly, civil conflicts are settled out of court.[94] Literature on bargaining and settlement has evolved in trying to explain the reasons for negotiation breakdown. In first instance, the purpose has been to explain this phenomenon based on unyielding parties. Later, the explanations focused on information asymmetries and cost burdens. Further analyses considered risk attitudes of parties, strategic aspects in negotiation, and the role of legal rules in the pre-trial settlement process.

Like in the previous stages of the decision-making process the parties involved base their decisions whether to settle or to sue on their individual cost-benefit analysis.[95] The main argument provided in the literature for having many conflicts resolved outside the court is grounded on the low transaction costs for settling compared to the high transaction costs for using the legal system.[96] A settlement can take place in every stage of the legal conflict: before the consult of a lawyer until right before the pronunciation of the verdict.[97] The settlement represents a co-operative resolution of the dispute, whereas the trial is a non-co-operative resolution.[98]

Based on behavioural economics and game theory,[99] we can get economic insights into the selection of conflicts that go to court. Economic theory suggests that both parties to a conflict are aware that they can gain a co-operative surplus if they settle. This surplus is the difference between the relatively low costs of negotiation and the high costs of trial.[100] Consequently, resolving a conflict by settling is thus more efficient than by trial.[101] The determinants of the behavioural approach are identical to the previous stage of conflict, namely the value at stake, the information with respect to the chance to prevail in court, and the private costs of a trial.[102] The higher the estimated chance of winning the case before court for the potential plaintiff, the stronger is his negotiating position in a settlement.[103]

94 Shavell 1997; Posner 2010; Cooter & Ulen 2011, p. 386.
95 Cooter & Rubinfeld 1989.
96 *Ibid.*; Posner 2010.
97 Posner 2010.
98 Cooter & Ulen 2011, p. 400.
99 Game theory deals with any situation where two or more *players* (*e.g.* plaintiff and defendant in a procedural setting) decide on their *strategies* (*e.g.* settle or trial, appeal or do not appeal). The *payoet seqs* generated by one player's strategy depend on the strategy chosen by the other player(s). Game theory is a valuable economic tool to deal with situations where different parties interact and has been applied, *inter alia*, in the economic analysis of contract law, competition law and procedural law.
100 Cooter & Ulen 2011, p. 400.
101 Landes 1971.
102 Cooter & Rubinfeld 1989; Landes 1971; Posner 1973.
103 Cooter & Ulen 2011, pp. 399-401.

The claim of the victim and the settlement offer of the injurer are determined by the net expected value of a possible trial.[104] For estimating the net expected benefit of trial it is important to specify the underlying *cost shifting rule, i.e.* each pays his own costs (the 'American system')[105] or loser pays all (the 'European system'). The net-expected benefit of a trial for the potential plaintiff consists of the expected value of the verdict multiplied by the chance to win the case, minus the costs of a trial. Under the European system the potential plaintiff subtracts the total private costs of a trial multiplied by the chance to that he will lose in court.[106] Under both the American and the European system, the value of the net-expected benefit of a trial determines the minimum accepted settlement offer by the potential plaintiff. On the other hand, the net-expected loss of the potential defendant due to a trial determines the maximum offer in a settlement.[107] Under the European system the total private costs would have to be subtracted, discounted by the chance to lose.[108]
We can expect a settlement if the net-expected loss of the potential defendant minus the net-expected benefit of the potential plaintiff leads to a positive value. In other words, if the maximum offer by the potential defendant exceeds the minimum accepted offer by the potential plaintiff. The settlement range depends on the individual estimations of both parties. The greater the range, the more likely settlement becomes.[109] Both parties can realise a financial gain if they succeed to avoid a trial, or, in other words, they would lose more in case a settlement is rejected. The concrete result of a settlement is dependent on the negotiation skills of the parties, but it will be a function of the assessment of the expected probability to win by the plaintiff.[110] A settlement fails if the potential plaintiff and the potential defendant expect to realise more advantages at court.[111] This means that the potential plaintiff expects a higher net benefit from trial compared to the settlement offer, and that the potential defendant expects a lower net-loss from trial.[112]
The more realistic the appraisal of the possible outcome of a trial, the more likely a settlement becomes.[113] A necessary condition for making realistic estimations is information.[114] Many authors see in asymmetric information the main reason for a breakdown of settlement negotiations.[115] But other factors might influence the negotiation positions

104 Cooter & Rubinfeld 1990; Posner 2010.
105 See also recent changes in the Irish legal system on environmental litigation: The Environment (Miscellaneous Provisions) Act 2011.
106 Posner 2010.
107 Cooter & Rubinfeld 1989.
108 Posner 2010.
109 Landes 1971.
110 *Ibid.*
111 Gravelle 1993; Posner 2010.
112 Gould 1973.
113 *Ibid.*; Zeisel, Kalven & Buchholz 1978.
114 Priest & Klein 1984.
115 Shavell 1999; Bebchuk 1984.

of the parties as well, such as risk attitude (risk aversion or risk loving), optimism and strategic behaviour.

4.3.4.2 Mediation

A tendency in environmental matters, which may also have its relevance in the framework of the Aarhus Convention, is mediation. The question is hence how one can view mediation in the light of the economic theory that has just been explained. The answer is, as may be clear from the previous analysis, nuanced.

From the perspective of the plaintiff, *i.e.* a member of the public seeking access to justice via administrative or judicial procedures, a mediation model has huge advantages. A similarity between settlement and mediation is that parties do not need to access the formal court system and try to reach an out-of-court settlement. Mediation can take various forms depending on the party acting as a mediator. The similarity with a settlement is that the goal is to stimulate negotiations between the parties involved in order to reach a solution (settlement) without the intervention of a court system.

In the introduction to this chapter we pointed out that the traditional economic models focus on a plaintiff-defendant relationship as between a victim and an injurer, whereas the situation in a typical *Aarhus*-case often concerns the relationship between a member of the public and a public authority.[116] However, the economic reasoning just presented perfectly applies to mediation in cases between a member of the public and public authorities in environmental matters. The primary reason for the plaintiff seeking access to environmental justice to be interested in mediation is obviously that this may entail lower costs and easier access. Depending upon the legal system involved (in this respect still important differences between the Member States exist), the access to justice of the Aarhus-type may require legal representation by a lawyer. That is, after all, an issue not directly regulated by the Aarhus Convention. For example, for a member of the public to have access to a judicial procedure against a private person (in the sense of Art 9(3) of the Aarhus Convention) many legal systems require representation by a lawyer. Again, very much depending upon the legal system involved, this may entail high costs for the member of the public.[117] The major advantage of mediation (although this may depend on who the mediator is) is that often no representation by a legal counsel is required and hence the costs involved are likely to be lower.

This immediately points at advantages of mediation also from a social perspective. There is quite a bit of experience with so-called consumer alternative dispute resolution, of which mediation is one type. These ADR models are often praised because they can lead to quick

116 See Section 4.2.

117 See on the costs for seeking access to justice the contributions in Tuil & Visser 2010 and see also Faure, Fernhout & Philipsen 2010.

decisions (compared to the traditional court system) and decisions can be reached at relatively low costs. The lower (administrative) costs of mediation systems result from (usually) lower evidentiary standards, while no professional lawyers are involved and no formal rules of legal procedure need to be applied. The flexibility of mediation hence can lead to low cost solutions. There is ample empirical evidence in the consumer ADR area that ADR and mediation lead to speedier decisions than the traditional court system.[118] Mediation is sometimes organised by private organisations and therefore may be linked to a scheme of self-regulation. To the extent that that is the case, the traditional advantages of self-regulation apply: lower administrative costs and information advantages of the organising body.[119] Self-regulation traditionally has an information advantage which may also play a role in case of environmental mediation. Mediators specialised in environmental matters may be better informed than general administrative or civil courts that would have to decide upon a Aarhus-conflict.[120] To the extent that mediators are privately organised they may also have better incentives for cost-reductions than civil or administrative courts who are often part of a (state) bureaucracy where incentives for court reduction may be lacking.[121]

However, ADR-type solutions like mediation do not only have advantages. The higher costs of the court system compared with that of ADR do have a reason: the higher evidentiary thresholds, involvement of professional lawyers and procedural rules all supposedly contribute to a higher quality of (environmental) decision-making. If these guarantees (and costs) would be reduced, decisions can be made more quickly and at lower costs, but the probability of 'wrong' decisions would increase. This is what economists refer to as *error costs*. Moreover, in the area of consumer ADR, lower thresholds in ADR systems (like mediation) have the substantial disadvantage of attracting frivolous suits.[122]

It follows from the above that the economic case for environmental mediation in Aarhus-type cases depends on the outcome of a cost-benefit analysis. If it can be argued that the savings in administrative and lawyer costs are larger than the potential error costs resulting from reduced procedural safeguards, environmental mediation may make sense. It is difficult to make general statements on the outcome of this balancing test, as it will depend upon the specifics of the case. It *can*, however, be argued that deciding on Aarhus-rights is certainly not an easy matter. Error costs should therefore be taken seriously. If a mediator would be highly specialised in cases related to the Aarhus Convention and the alternative would be a general (civil or administrative) court that is not specialised, mediation may

118 See in that respect inter alia the recent volume by Hodges, Benöhr & Kreutzfeldt-Banda 2012.

119 See generally on these advantages of self-regulation, Ogus 1995, 2000. In the context of the legal professions see also Philipsen 2010.

120 Obviously the case would be different if the court would not be a general one but a specialised environmental court in which case the court may have an equal expertise in environmental matters as an environmental mediator. See on the advantages of specialised environmental courts Pring & Pring 2010.

121 Although with decreasing public budgets also court systems increasingly have incentives for cutting costs.

122 See on that issue Weber 2012.

be attractive. If that is not the case, the error costs created through mediation are likely to outweigh the costs of the court system. Hence, whether environmental mediation is desirable to a large extent depends on who the mediator would be and whether there is a specialised court dealing with Aarhus-type cases.
A final aspect that has to be considered is that when mediation in this context is only voluntary, it may not necessarily be effective. The public authority may, as practice shows, lack the incentive to participate in mediation if participation is not mandatory.

4.3.5 *Effects of Law on Behaviour*

The litigation strategy of individuals is influenced by many factors, including the prevailing legal rules, availability and relevance of evidence, requirements of the procedure, and court delay. A change in any of these factors may cause a multitude of effects. This requires a deeper analysis to understand the decisions made by (potential) litigating parties, in order to prevent (as much as possible) effects that are inefficient.[123]

4.3.5.1 Costs

If the legislator takes measures that affect the costs of suing and going to trial, the net-expected value of a suit for parties involved in a dispute will change as well. This affects negotiations before a court trial since the expectations regarding a possible trial will be reflected in the offered, respectively accepted, compensation for damage. Higher charges for using the public court system will in general lead to an increase in the settlement offer and a decrease in the value accepted by the potential defendant. This increases the likelihood of an out-of-court settlement, because the net value of the suit decreases while the net loss of a trial for the potential defendant increases.[124]

It is useful, however, to make a distinction between the effects on the opponents in a litigation process. Several Law and Economics scholars have argued that higher court fees will decrease the minimum accepted settlement offer of the damaged party, while the effect on the causer is ambiguous (depending on whether or not there is an effect on the probability to prevail in court).[125]

4.3.5.2 Burden of Proof

The burden of proof determines which party has to submit evidence in a trial. The burden of proof can be imposed on the plaintiff, *e.g.* in negligence accusations, or on the

123 Posner 1973, p. 420.
124 Landes 1971, p. 418.
125 Bebchuk 1984, pp. 409-410.

defendant, *e.g.* if he or she must prove that the plaintiff acted negligently. Procedural law determines a minimum standard of submitted evidence. In the US and Great Britain the plaintiff has to submit proofs of preponderance of evidence. Under the continental law system usually a proof beyond reasonable doubt is required.[126] Imposing a burden of proof on the parties leads to costs, and the stricter those burdens are, the higher the costs. The goal for social welfare is to minimise the sum of error costs of the judicial decisions and private investments in providing evidence. In addition, legal rules should provide incentives to choose an optimal level of precaution to avoid a legal conflict. However, there exist requirements concerning the burden of proof beyond economic reasoning, such as requirements of justice and fairness.[127]

4.3.5.3 Claim for Compensation

Any change in the legal requirements for compensation damage affects the basic conditions of the estimation of the net expected benefit or loss of a court trial. The value at stake increases and this affects the settlement negotiations.[128] In addition, optimism may influence negotiations negatively, by making negotiations fail more often, ending up in trial. On the other hand, trials become more expensive and more risky due to an increased value at stake, which leads to the opposite effect (successful negotiations) if parties are risk averse.[129]

4.3.5.4 Information Asymmetries

Any voluntarily exchange of information can increase the probability of settlement since it helps to adjust estimations, by reducing unjustified optimism. If no legal procedure regarding the disclosure of information exists, it is likely that the parties bring in strategic aspects. Parties will rather withhold advantageous information in order to use it in trial.[130] Expectations regarding the value and probability of a verdict affect the result of negotiations out of court, but not its optimum.[131] Legal procedures should aim at an optimisation of information exchange. The question arises to what extent an obligated exchange of information is necessary to attain this goal. The direct sub-goal is to reduce unjustified optimism and pessimism among litigating parties to reach legal certainty and the probability of an out-of-court settlement.[132] There are also arguments against an obligated exchange

126 Cooter & Ulen 2011, pp. 458-459. This does not hold for the Netherlands, where the party with the burden of proof has to provide proof that his version of the facts is the most plausible.

127 Epstein 1973, p. 152.

128 Danzon & Lillard 1983 found that in case higher compensation payments are to be expected due to a judgement, the probability that the parties will end up in a trial will become larger.

129 Cooter & Rubinfeld 1989.

130 Posner 1973, p. 423.

131 Gould 1973.

132 Posner 1973, p. 423.

of information, because this procedure generates costs in the beginning of a litigation process. Significant costs of information disclosure in relation to the compensation can lead to the fact that the victim refrains from bringing a suit.[133]

In this respect we can refer to what was mentioned above about litigation as a mechanism to disclose information.[134] In addition we can refer again to Article 9(5) of the Aarhus Convention, which imposes a legal obligation on Member States to disseminate information on access to justice rules. Article 9(5) can, in the light of the discussion here, clearly be considered as a mechanism to reduce information asymmetries.

4.3.6 Trial

The previous sections analysed the decisions made by litigating parties in settlement negotiations. If settlement negotiations fail, usually a trial follows. The hybrid model of Cooter and Rubinfeld concludes that a trial follows a failed attempt to settle, if the minimum accepted offer for compensation of the damaged party is higher than the maximum offer of the damaging party.[135] In this case the settlement range is negative and an agreement (in the form of a settlement) becomes impossible. Both parties expect a verdict to be in their advantage. In this section the behaviour of the parties in the last phase of the legal conflict (*i.e.* the trial) will be discussed.[136]

The expected benefit of a trial in court is determined by the nature of the case, but also by the underlying procedural law. Legal provisions on the burden of proof, the reasoning of proof, damage estimation, etc., determine the effort that parties must undertake to maximise their benefits. All efforts made by parties in order to present their case are going hand in hand with higher costs, which diminish the expected benefit of a trial. Parties therefore have to balance costs and benefits of further investments in a litigation process.[137]

It should be noted that higher investments in litigating also give signals to the judge, because judges are aware of the fact that collecting information is expensive and therefore probably advantageous to the party. This motivates litigating parties to invest more in lawyers, experts and evidence.[138] It may, however, also lead to strategic behaviour.

Addressing the decision-making of litigating parties in Aarhus-litigation more specifically, we need to remember the discussion presented in Section 4.3.4 on settlement and

133 Kobayashi & Parker (2000).

134 See Section 4.2.2.2.

135 Cooter & Rubinfeld 1989.

136 Cooter & Rubinfeld 1990, p. 539.

137 This is based on the assumption that the investment is positively correlated with the probability of success before court. See Posner 1973; Tullock 1980; Wittman 1988; Katz 1987; Cooter & Rubinfeld 1989; Hay 1995; Kobayashi & Parker 2000.

138 Cooter & Rubinfeld 1989.

mediation. The cost-benefit analysis that parties make related to the question whether to engage in a trial (*e.g.* to obtain injunctive relief in an environmental case), needs to incorporate also the costs and benefits of alternatives such as settlement and ADR. The higher the stakes are in litigation, the higher investments and costs of formal litigation, and the more attractive alternatives may become. In this respect we can refer to the trade-offs discussed in 4.3.4.

4.3.7 *Standing and Access to Justice*

When starting an economic analysis of (increased) access to justice, it is useful, as a background, to explain why a (widened) access to justice may be effective from an economic perspective. The starting point is that private law remedies to be used by individual victims like in classic tort or nuisance cases may not work in environmental cases. Shavell offers many reasons why private enforcement of environmental standards may not work: the damage may be too widespread, resulting in low damage amounts to individual victims even if the totality of the damages is very high.[139] These circumstances produce, in the words of Schäfer, a "rational apathy" on the part of the individual victims.[140] Therefore, none of them are motivated to take on the expense of litigation. Moreover, a private law suit may never be brought due to problems of causation or latency, which is characterised by long time lapse between the emission and the actual occurrence of the harm.[141] These problems are especially prevalent in environmental cases. Moreover, collective litigation does not always follow either, since the transaction costs for the group to get organised can in some cases be high.[142] This may be an argument in favour of allowing a lower threshold for *locus standi* in case of environmental harm and even allowing the development of so-called environmental PIL.[143]

Before addressing the rationale for (in some particular cases) widening access to justice (via environmental PIL) first we need to address the economic justification for the traditional legal standing requirement. The basic rationale is that parties should only be able to sue when they have a direct interest at stake for damages they have personally suffered.[144] Traditionally, *locus standi* is an admissibility condition that acts as a gatekeeper for the filing of cases.[145] A central issue of the standing doctrine is that a plaintiff should indicate an injury and, moreover, which substantive rights were violated.

---

139 Shavell 1984, pp. 372-374.

140 Schäfer 2000.

141 See Kaplow 1986 and Faure & Fenn 1999.

142 Schäfer 2000.

143 See on environmental PIL in India Faure & Raja 2010. See also Chapter 5 of this report.

144 Divan & Rosencranz 2001, p. 137.

145 Van Aaken 2005.

The traditional economic argument against expanding standing contents that it would lead to many inefficient procedures, resulting in an inefficient use of the court system and potentially to over-deterrence. A distinction should in that respect, however, be made between *locus standi* in private law and in public law. A strict *locus standi* in private law may make sense from an economic perspective in order not to overburden courts and not to create overdeterrence of operators. However, the argument may be different in public law, such as *e.g.* in judicial review cases and in common law public nuisance cases.[146] There are various approaches to understanding why the standing requirement may not always work in the interest of justice (and hence why enlarged standing and access to justice should be considered).

In this respect we can recall the discussion on collective redress above[147] where we indicated that especially in environmental cases damage may often have a widespread nature as a result of which the private incentive to bring (Aarhus-)litigation may be too limited. That is precisely an economic justification, not only for a widened access to justice, but also for either collective redress mechanisms (in case of widespread losses) or environmental PIL. In that sense environmental PIL (*e.g.* granting standing to environmental NGOs based on the Aarhus Convention) can, from an economic perspective, be considered as an essential instrument to deal with cases of environmental harm where the losses to individual victims would be relatively low as a result of which private incentives to litigate (*e.g.* suing for injunctive relief) may be limited.

The first approach to standing and access to justice hence follows from a pure rational choice (economic) perspective: apart from the problem of 'rational disinterest', discussed earlier, the verdict in a case with a large number of stakeholders takes on the nature of a public good, which would not be provided for, or risk, at best, undersupplied by a rational victim.[148] In that case, *locus standi* can become an impediment to the redress process. A similar failure could occur where the affected population has no judicial access.

A second approach has been presented from a justice standpoint. Since, judicial review, broadly defined, is the power of a court to review the actions of public sector bodies in terms of their legality or constitutionality, it becomes imperative to have a mechanism that accomplishes this.[149] A broadened access to justice (and more particularly environmental PIL) can be seen as one way of bringing the courts the claims of unlawful exercise of power or violation of rights by a government entity. This broader notion of access to justice and more particularly PIL, will be further discussed in Chapter 5. At this point it is important to recall that a broadened access to justice cannot only be justified from a social justice

146 Stein 1979.

147 See Section 4.3.4.3.

148 Van Aaken 2005, p. 50. See also Section 4.1.1.

149 See broadly the contributions in Seerden 2007 and in Seerden, Heldeweg & Deketelaere 2002.

perspective, but also from an economic perspective as a tool to internalise environmental externalities.

4.4 Applied to the Four Options

In this section we will apply the economic insights presented above to the four options laid out in Chapter 3. The crucial question thereby is how the various costs for the stakeholders involved relate to a change from the status quo to other options. Of course, a full-fledged cost-benefit analysis cannot be provided for the simple reason that data on those costs are generally not available and would require a micro-level study of Member States. Even for individual Member States, there may only be some general sense of costs of access to justice, but no detailed information that allows for a serious quantitative study. Hence, we will merely indicate how the various options affect the costs of the different stakeholders involved and make a qualitative estimation.

One additional reason for the estimation to be of a rather descriptive and qualitative nature (instead of providing a quantitative analysis) is that, as the description of the four options made clear, the actual costs involved for the stakeholders will to a large extent today still depend upon Member State law. There are indeed substantial differences between the Member States as has also been indicated in earlier research.[150]

Earlier, we distinguished four groups of stakeholders of which the incentives would be affected resulting from changes in access to justice:

1. Potential plaintiffs: individuals and (environmental) NGOs;[151]
2. Potential defendants: operators;[152]
3. Administrative authorities whose decisions would be challenged (this also includes the institutions, both at Member State and EU level);
4. The courts that may be confronted with increasing suits.

150 See *e.g.* De Sadeleer, Roller & Dross 2002.

151 In some cases NGOs can be defendants, for instance if there is an appeal at second instance against decisions positive for NGOs (business can then become plaintiffs). We do not deal with this situation in the analysis below.

152 For the purposes of this analysis, we refer to the defendants here as the operators, in other words, enterprises who would *e.g.* seek a permit. Of course we are aware that in an administrative decision it is not an enterprise who is the defendant but rather the public authority whose decision is challenged. Art 9(3) of the Aarhus Convention refers explicitly to both by mentioning administrative or judicial procedures to challenge acts and omissions by private persons and public authorities. For reasons of analytical simplicity we have divided the stakeholders in (2) the potential defendants, in this case meaning operators (enterprises) and (3) the administrative authorities whose decisions would be challenged, realising of course that in an administrative suit they could be defendants as well.

In addition to these four "direct" stakeholders we tentatively add the fifth (and potentially most important) stakeholder, being the environment. The broader goal of the Aarhus Convention and obviously of the environmental acquis is environmental protection or, if one wishes to formulate it in access terms, access to natural resources. Therefore we will attempt to indicate the effects of the four options on the environment, although admittedly this is rather speculative. It does, however, follow from the economic analysis presented in this chapter that access to justice is necessary also in the view of providing a better environmental protection. Hence, as a rough proxy it can be argued that better (also in the sense of providing more certainty) access to justice will also increase environmental protection.[153]

It should be stressed from the outset that the nature of the costs to which these four stakeholders are involved are different. The costs incurred by administrative authorities and institutions (3) and the courts (4) can be considered as social costs, whereas the costs incurred by potential plaintiffs (1) and potential defendants (2) are rather private costs. However, there is, at least from an economic perspective, no reason not to take private costs into account in the calculus as well.

Let us now address the four options in more detail by simply referring to the analysis above on the consequences of the four options and the changes this would probably bring in access to justice. We will use the economic framework concerning the effects of various rules on the behaviour of the parties concerned to verify how the various options would affect the incentives of the four groups of stakeholders we just identified.

4.4.1 Option 1: Business as Usual – Soft Law Approach

As was mentioned above, this option would imply that the policy maker would only work towards the implementation of the Aarhus Convention, but not take further substantial action. This would, as was made clear above, *inter alia* imply:

- that an appeal/review procedure would not be introduced in countries where this does not yet exist;
- the procedure for the recognition of entities which aim to protect the environment would not be introduced;
- existing gaps in the transposition and application of Article 9(3) of the Aarhus Convention would remain.

153 For a full economic appreciation, this increased environmental protection (*i.e.* the benefits in environmental protection) should be weighed against the marginal costs to get the full picture on social costs.

If one would assess the general effects for the stakeholders involved of this option, we can be relatively brief:

- for both courts and administrative authorities this will (as is the case today) to a large extent depend upon Member State law and the same is basically the case for the private entities (potential plaintiffs and potential defendants);
- this of course implies that, in Member States where the access to justice for citizens and NGOs is currently relatively low, the expected costs for potential defendants are lower than under the other three options, whereas the expected costs for potential plaintiffs are higher.

Looking at social costs, this option would have the disadvantage of:

- remaining high uncertainty (which may also lead to private costs for *e.g.* operators), more particularly concerning the question to what extent Member State law already complies as much as possible with Article 9(3) of the Aarhus Convention;
- potentially higher costs for Member States and potential plaintiffs, due to the non-action by the Commission;
- possible social (external) costs related to environmental damage that is not internalised.

A consequence of remaining differences between the Member States and remaining uncertainty would be that no level playing field is created.
A more detailed estimation reflecting on the theoretical bases developed in the previous sections will observe every party involved separately.

Plaintiffs

Individuals: this option does not lead to legal certainty in the form of an EU level minimum standard. This means that in some Member States individuals are not likely to claim damages in relation to environmental harm. The risks or costs of suing may be too high, or individuals simply lack standing.

NGOs: having access to justice by NGOs may help creating precedents and hence some basis that the courts can rely on in solving environmental cases. NGOs can help to improve the law and reduce social costs if they bring suit in cases where individuals face a 'rational apathy' problem (see Section 4.3.7). However, option 1 means that existing differences between Member States regarding access to justice by NGOs will remain. NGOs seeking to bring an environmental case before court in countries with restricted or disputed access may have to incur costs not on the subject matter itself, *i.e.* the environmental damage, but on being allowed as a litigating party. This leads to further legal uncertainty and public costs for using the courts.

Defendants
In this situation defendants cannot estimate the net expected costs of a trial correctly. This has different effects. On the one hand a potential defendant is not able to optimise his precaution level, and will also not be able to make efficient decisions with respect to production and investments. On the other hand, this legal uncertainty leads to a source of strategic behaviour or even strategic use of public courts.

Institutions
A task of ministries or administrative agencies in individual Member States could consist of collecting data and information about case law and make it available to all interested entities of the society. This would involve costs that are relatively low.
Costs for the Commission under this option are limited also, as they would only consist of formulating some form of commentary or guidelines explaining the significance and implications of the Treaty provisions and case law.[154]

Courts
In Member States with restricted access to justice in environmental matters, the number of suits may be inefficiently low from a social welfare perspective. This legal uncertainty is likely to lead to external costs, as discussed in Section 4.2. Strategic behavior by defendants may also lead to inefficiently high social and court costs.
In Member States with wide access to justice, strategic behaviour by plaintiffs may lead to social and court costs. However, differences between option 1 and the other options are expected to be relatively low in these countries.

Environment
This situation may not be ideal for the environment given:
- remaining high uncertainty;
- desirable litigation against environment-damaging activity, that is not exercised;
- and hence potential external costs related to environmental damage that are not internalised.

4.4.2 Option 2: Addressing Existing Gaps in Member States Provisions

As far as costs are concerned, option 2 (infringement procedures) would imply that the European Commission takes action against those Member States of which it is held that their national law does not comply with the requirements of Article 9(3) of the Aarhus

154 Specifications to Invitation to Tender DG ENV.A.2/ETU/2012/0009rl, p. 3.

Convention as interpreted in the case law. The legal basis for this would be that the Commission has an obligation to bring infringement cases based on the fact that the Aarhus Convention is part of EU law and the Commission is the Guardian of the Treaties. As Guardian the Commission would hence bring legal action against Member States that do not comply with the Aarhus convention.

This option may obviously create rather substantial costs for the European Commission. A study on the costs of not implementing the environmental *acquis* provided some indication of those costs, mentioning especially that costs are not only incurred by the Commission, but also by the Member States concerned. Infringement procedures lead to *direct costs* (time spent by both the Commission and Member States officials and legal fees) and *indirect costs* (such as the disruption of normal work assignments for the involved officials and the knock-on effects on other policies as they are not being looked after while the case is ongoing).[155] The study indicates that the most significant costs of infringement cases is not the amount of man-days spent to deal with the case, but the fact that a case interrupts the normal working routines if it implies that certain key staff for a longer period of time is committed to these cases. This is especially a significant cost for the affected Member State, but it can equally be a cost for the European Commission itself. Hence, one can certainly not argue that the option of bringing cases is costless; compared with option 1, it can therefore be held that option 2 creates significant costs.

In addition to both the European Commission and the involved Member State incurring costs as a result of the procedure, there are costs for those Member States who are forced to *adapt national legislation* according to the outcome of the case. Moreover, when the case is lost, fines could be imposed on the Member State. However, the adaptation costs of national legislation can be ignored, since those are costs that the Member State should incur in any event, and particularly also under options 3 and 4.

As far as the direct stakeholders are involved, it is probably important to briefly recall the implications of some of the cases we referred to in Chapter 2 to assess how this may affect incentives of stakeholders and hence to which type of additional costs it could potentially lead:

- The *Trianel* case implied that NGOs promoting environmental protection can have access to justice even where, on the grounds that the rules relied on protect only the interest of the general public and not the interest of the individuals, national procedural law does not permit this.
- The *Janecek* case came to a similar conclusion with respect to individuals, using a wide interpretation of the concept of an impairment of a right.

Both cases may hence (depending upon national law in the Member States) lead to more access to justice for individuals and/or NGOs. This is especially true for Germany and Austria.

155 See the costs of not implementing the environmental *acquis* (2011), appendix F1, pp. 163-164.

The reason is not only that both cases concerned preliminary questions of German judges, but also that Germany and Austria have a rights-based system of judicial protection.

- The *Slovak* case held that Article 9(3) of the Aarhus Convention should be interpreted to the fullest extent possible in order to enable environmental protection organisations to challenge administrative decisions before a court. The precise consequence of this decision is debated. Some scholars hold that the consequence of this decision is that Article 9(3) of the Aarhus Convention is applicable (*i.e.* access should be granted) across the full breadth of European environmental law.[156]

This seems to be a very broad interpretation of this decision which, as we argued above, could also be seen otherwise. Depending upon the interpretation of the *Slovak* case, it would hence apply a still broader access to justice than currently awarded under Directive 2003/35 (limited to cases falling under the EIA and IPPC Directives). If one were to follow the interpretation of *e.g.* Jans and Vedder, the consequence of the *Slovak* case would be a general access to justice in environmental matters according to Article 9(3) of the Aarhus Convention, beyond only those cases falling under the EIA and the IPPC Directives. Under that interpretation the access to justice would be substantially enlarged.

What would the consequences of the Commission pursuing compliance with this case law according to option 2 imply for the stakeholders involved?

This question is not that easy to answer since, as we made clear, different interpretations exist concerning the precise implications of the case law. However, a result from *Trianel* and *Janecek* may be that in Member States where this would not already be the case, NGOs promoting environmental protection and individuals can have access to justice. However, it is important to remember that the importance of the *Trianel* case[157] is restricted to the interpretation of Directive 2003/35 (allowing public participation in EIA and IPPC procedures). Hence, the marginal (additional) costs for stakeholders as a result of the implementation of those two cases may be limited and will apply only for those Member States that do not yet grant access to justice as required by this case law. As far as the *Slovak case* is concerned, the consequences could be larger if one were to follow its broad interpretation that Article 9(3) of the Aarhus Convention would be applicable across the full breadth of European environmental law. This is also the interpretation that the Commission gives to this case, as indicated by Communication 95/2012 and the terms of reference for the current study. This means that indeed the result of the *Slovak* case would imply an obligation to provide full access to justice under the full breadth of the EU environmental acquis. That would substantially increase the scope of access to justice. Hence, the consequences for the stakeholders in Member States depend strongly upon existing law in Member States (and more particularly whether this already complies with the CJEU case

156 See Jans & Vedder 2012, p. 237.

157 The *Janecek* case applied to air quality plants.

law) and the particular way in which one interprets the CJEU case law. Given the Commission's interpretation of the *Slovak* case this also implies that a substantial number of infringement cases could be brought by the Commission if no EU law would be adopted in this area.

Looking at the particular stakeholders, one could therefore hold that social costs for administrative authorities and courts could increase slightly if the Commission were to pursue implementation on the basis of the *Trianel* and *Janecek* cases, but then only for those Member States that are not in compliance yet; the marginal costs may be more substantial if the Commission were to follow a broad interpretation of the *Slovak* case.

The theoretical outcomes based on the welfare and behavioral approach will now again be reflected on the stakeholders separately.

Plaintiffs

Individuals: under this option legal certainty could improve, because of the information that becomes available through the infringement procedures. If so, potential plaintiffs can make better decisions concerning the chance to prevail in court and costs of litigation. The number of suits is expected to increase in the direction of the 'optimal' level of litigation, but the optimum is not likely to be reached by this option, since a relatively high level of legal uncertainty remains.

NGOs: as for individuals, uncertainty with respect to acceptance before court and the legal situation remains and is likely to result in a number of suits lower than the optimal level. It is even possible that the CJEU procedures may lead to a second flood of suits and hence increase private (and social) costs of trials.

Defendants

A level playing field will not be realised by this option. The decisions on precaution, production and investments, though, are likely to move towards an optimal point. But inefficiencies still remain, since the expected costs of this option are very dependent on the outcome of the infringement procedures and the current state of Member State law. The possibility for defendants of using the public courts for strategic purposes still remains.

As will also be explained when referring to the institutions (3), this option still entails substantial uncertainty and possibilities of (European) litigation. Given the uncertainty there is even the risk that some projects may be stopped until the CJEU has ruled on specific interpretations. This could cause serious costs for business.

Institutions

It is possible that costs will have to be incurred by those Member States that – according to the Commission – have not implemented in their national laws the essence of the recent

CJEU case law. Costs for the Commission itself will increase to some extent due to the infringement procedures. As indicated above, this includes both direct and indirect (opportunity) costs. Some social costs due to legal uncertainty may remain.
It should also be repeated that this option entails the risk of a flood of cases for two reasons: given the Commission's interpretation of the *Slovak* case there is a danger of many infringement cases against all Member States that have not provided access to justice under the full breadth of the EU environmental acquis. Second, given the uncertainty there may be a flood of suits from national judges by preliminary references asking for interpretations on procedural aspects, for example what should be considered as timely, not costly, what is precisely injunctive relief in relation to Article 9(3) and the standing requirements of the *Slovak brown bear* case.

Courts
An increasing workload for the CJEU and Member States courts can be expected.
The conclusion is hence that this option may again lead to additional costs, but that the precise scope of those costs is difficult to predict since it strongly depends on Member State law. Moreover, there are uncertainties as far as the interpretation of the case law is concerned and finally one should also take into account that there are still a few pending infringement cases of which the outcome is uncertain. Given these uncertainties, this option would hence, as was the case with option 1, not create a level playing field.

Environment
This option may be better than option (1) for the environment, depending on the number of cases and their outcomes. However, there still is substantial uncertainty and the final scope of environmental protection may have to wait for a long period depending upon final decisions by the CJEU.

4.4.3 Option 3: Making a New Proposal

The third option would be not to rely any longer on COM(2003) 624 but to rather introduce a new legislative proposal which would basically implement emerging case law as just sketched in option 2. This could either take the form of a completely new proposal or of substantially modifying the old proposal COM(2003) 624.
As far as the consequences for stakeholders are concerned, we can be relatively brief. Both for social as well as private costs the consequences would be similar to those just sketched for option 2.[158] However, there would be some significant differences in the sense that a

158 See Section 4.4.2.

new proposal would create more legal certainty and hence there would be less need for litigation compared to option 2. Litigation costs would then be substantially lower.

An important difference would be that the proposed directive would force the Member States to apply Article 9(3) Aarhus Convention and to grant *locus standi* for citizens and NGOs in environmental cases which do not fall under the IPPC or EIA Directives. Whether this is a significant difference compared with option 2 depends on the interpretation of the *Slovak* case. As stated in 4.4.2, some scholars argue that already now access to justice for NGOs must be granted in all Member States with regard to all environmental cases. If this opinion is followed, option 3 does not differ much from option 2 and costs would be largely comparable. However, if access to court for NGOs can only be granted when the statutes of a Member State can be interpreted in accordance with Article 9(3) Aarhus Convention, option 3 would make a significant difference. Access to justice for NGOs will have to be granted in all environmental cases, even in countries whose statutes at present cannot be interpreted in accordance with Article 9(3). However, there is another substantial advantage of option 3 that should be mentioned. Since only the *Slovak* case dealt with the interpretation of Article 9(3), one cannot argue that there is an established and clear case law providing an equivocal information to stakeholders. Stakeholders like NGOs today still have to fight for their right in national courts if these would not follow the broad interpretation of the mentioned cases. Also the Commission has to take strong action under option 2. Therefore, both for NGOs and the Commission there would be substantial advantages to option 3: the uncertainty that still would exist under option 2, as well as the substantial costs of infringement procedures, would disappear.

Instead of the costs of infringement procedures (under option 2), there would be the costs of drafting the new directive, but these can be assumed not to be substantially higher than the costs of all the infringement procedures against those Member States that would not yet be in compliance with CJEU case law. However, there may be enforcement costs related to insufficient implementation (or enforcement) of the new directive in particular Member States.

A major advantage of this option for stakeholders would be that there could be common benefits for business and NGOs (hence for the stakeholders involved) in the sense of timely procedures, procedural guarantees and increased legal certainty.

Looking again at the groups of stakeholders from an economic perspective:

Plaintiffs

Individuals: this option comes close to the creation of legal certainty (but only if the new directive does not create new legal questions). Potential defendants will be able to estimate the risk of suing correctly and hence come to efficient decisions. The number of suits will (in theory) tend to be optimal.

NGOs: legal certainty can be improved by allowing NGOs standing in environmental cases, in case of damage that is too low for individuals to have a credible suit due to rational apathy. Causers of damage will then be forced to internalise these external costs to society. If the law is clear the number of suits by NGOs should not increase, but will move towards the optimal number of suits that aim at reducing legal uncertainty or judgmental errors.

Defendants

The level playing field in the form of EU level minimum standards created by the new directive may provide (more) legal certainty to potential defendants and may hence lead to optimal decisions on their part (investments in safety and pollution abatement, materials used in production, etc.). If so, industry will be better able to internalise the external effects of environmental harm into their calculations. Strategic behaviour is expected to reduce if (and only if) the new law is indeed clear and a level playing field is created.

Institutions

There will be costs of formulating and implementing the directive, for the Commission and Member States, respectively. There will also be a need for communication about this directive. It may be estimated, though, that in the long run these costs will be lower than the total social costs of legal uncertainty, not implementing legal standards, and separate court proceedings.

There may also be additional costs for the Parties to the Aarhus Convention if they do not implement Article 9(3) in an appropriate manner.

Courts

The advantage of this option is that it can create legal certainty. This may have an effect on the number of suits in the sense that there will be less preliminary references as the acquis is already clear as it is based on case law developments of Directive 2003/35/EC in the context of public participation and access to justice. If legal certainty is created, suits on the interpretation of access to justice will no longer be needed.

However, given that the new directive would clarify access to justice one could argue that the number of cases filed by NGOs, giving clarity concerning the standing would increase (in economic terms it would move to the optimal number). In other words, the number of suits by NGOs may increase. But, as has been repeatedly stated in the economic analysis, that should not (necessarily) be considered as problematic, but in fact could be a desirable consequence compared to the status quo where there may be a suboptimal amount of Aarhus-litigation.

A final point to be made as far as courts are concerned, is that a new directive may include a provision on environmental mediation. If environmental mediation were to be introduced as an alternative to resolving Aarhus-disputes this could obviously reduce the case load and hence costs for courts.[159]

Environment

This option may (depending upon the final contents of the new proposal) have positive consequences for the environment. It can create more certainty as a result of which more (Aarhus)litigation is brought, leading to a better internalisation of external costs caused by environmental damage. From an environmental perspective option 3 hence seems to be preferred to options 1 and 2.

Summarising the above, we can state that to a large extent, this option 3 would be similar to option 2, with, however, a few important positive differences:

- The uncertainties which still exist in option 2 because of differences in interpretation of the case law and because of uncertainties concerning the outcome of pending infringement cases would in this option disappear. The costs of uncertainty would hence be reduced, provided that the new directive does not create new questions of interpretation and uncertainty;
- The existing differences in Member States (which would potentially still continue to exist also when pursuing option 2) would disappear as well since the directive would to a certain extent create a new harmonised system;
- As the scope of administrative decisions which will fall under the directive will be more targeted than in option 4, there will be less uncertainty about the question which decisions or omissions can be challenged before a court. This will, compared to option 4, reduce uncertainty and hence reduce costs of all stakeholders;
- Different from option 2, in this option the level playing field for stakeholders (more particularly the private actors (potential plaintiffs and defendants) could hence be more likely;
- Depending on whether the proposal would consider to introduce environmental mediation as an option court costs could decrease;
- Environmental effects in this option are better than in options 1 and 2.

4.4.4 *Option 4: Retain COM(2003) 624*

As we discussed above, there are a few noteworthy elements in this option which could lead to a substantial enlargement of access to justice:

- Article 4 of the proposal transposes the requirement of Article 9(3) of the Aarhus Convention ensuring that members of the public have access to justice to challenge

159 See on the trade-off between litigation and mediation Section 4.3.4.2.

the procedural and substantive legality of all kinds of administrative acts or omissions which may breach environmental law. Until now, Directive 2003/35/EC requires Member States only to ensure access to justice in cases falling under the EIA Directive or the IPPC Directive. This could hence substantially broaden the scope of access to justice, but again, this would depend on Member State law. For Member States where (like in Directive 2003/35/EC access to justice is only awarded in cases falling under the EIA or the IPPC Directive) this would lead to a substantial enlargement; in Member States where access to justice is more generally awarded in environmental cases, this would make less of a difference. It should be noted again that a similar article would be included in a new or substantially modified Directive, so there is no difference in this respect with option 3;

- Article 5 of the proposal requires standing of "qualified entities" in all kind of "environmental proceedings" while Directive 2003/35/EC would require standing for such entities only in procedures covered by the IPPC or the EIA Directive. Like in the situation with Article 4, the question whether this brings substantial additional access to justice (and hence potential additional costs) depends on whether the law of the Member States already provides such an access to the court in accordance with Article 9(3) of the Aarhus Convention;
- As the scope of the proposed directive is very broad and the kind of administrative acts falling under the directive are not at all limited, the new directive may cause discussion and uncertainty on what kind of acts and omissions it will be applying. If so, this uncertainty creates additional costs;
- As we mentioned above, the potentially most far reaching element in COM(2003) 624 is to be found in Articles 6 and 8 of the proposal. The reason is that this even goes beyond the Aarhus Convention and hence goes further than any of the other options discussed so far. It requires that those having legal standing according to Articles 4 (members of the public) or 5 (qualified entities) would also have access to an objection procedure within the administration. The competent administrative authority would have to decide within 12 weeks on such an objection. Article 8 regulates the procedure to recognise entities which have the objective to protect the environment. This also goes beyond the Aarhus Convention in the sense that a more minimalistic approach would be considered as compliant as well.

Again, the impact for stakeholders depends of course on Member State law:

- Articles 3, 4 and 5 of the proposal arguably transpose existing requirements of Article 9(3) Aarhus Convention. To the extent Member States already comply with those requirements, it makes no difference for the situation of stakeholders. To the extent this is not the case, it may lead to additional access and hence to additional costs. The situation is in that respect again comparable to option 2 which would address

existing gaps on the basis of Article 9(3) Aarhus Convention. However, in option 2 these existing gaps are addressed via infringement procedures (hence creating costs and uncertainty) whereas in this option these gaps are addressed via a directive.
- An important difference with option 2 would be that more legal certainty would be created. Moreover, the Commission would no longer need to bring infringement suits as a result of which those costs would be reduced.

However, the requirement of an appeal/review procedure and the introduction of a procedure to recognise entities which aim to protect the environment (Arts 6 and 8-9) go beyond the requirements of Article 9(3) of the Aarhus Convention and hence beyond any of the other options discussed so far. Again, to the extent Member States already have such a procedure,[160] this may not create additional costs, but to the extent this is not the case, it certainly will.
Like in option 3 it can be argued that there are common benefits for all stakeholders (NGOs and enterprises) in the form of timely procedures, procedural guarantees and legal certainty. However, a potentially problematic aspect of option 4 is that it does not build on existing case law of the CJEU, but new rules are created. This could potentially lead to new procedures.
Looking again at the stakeholder groups individually:

Plaintiffs
Individuals: decisions on bringing suit under this option are likely to be similar to option 3. Although more damage claims may be subject of a suit, the decisions still underlie a particular rationality. An increase of suits on the part of individuals is not expected, but cannot be fully excluded.
NGOs: environmental NGOs may increase the number of claims to put pressure on potential polluters or administrations (strategic behaviour). Apart from that, effects are expected to be similar to option 3.

Defendants
Defendants may (if legal uncertainties arise due to the broad scope of the directive) be over-deterred under this option. If so, this leads to potential defendants choosing an inefficiently high level of precaution and it will also affect their decision-making in production and investments to a possible sub-optimal level.

160 In most Member States review procedures do in fact already exist, as a result of which no additional costs would be incurred.

Institutions

The costs mentioned under option 3 are also relevant here. However, as mentioned above, in this scenario costs for institutions could be higher since the new set of rules would imply the necessity to launch perhaps new infringement procedures and the need for the (European) court to answer new preliminary references.

Courts

If there would be an increase in the number of suits because of claims by NGOs (which may be desirable from an economic perspective, see Section 4.4.3), this implies a higher workload for public courts, involving public (social) costs. The possibility of increased suing by individuals cannot be excluded entirely either.

Environment

More legal certainty is created and hence (desirable) Aarhus-litigation can be expected, leading to internalisation of external costs caused by environmental damage. The environmental effects of this option can be presumed to be the same as in option 3.

Summarising the discussion above, the following points emerge:

- Like option 3, this option would reduce costs of uncertainty by introducing a new directive; differences between existing Member State law would be reduced and a level playing field would be created.
- However, compared to option 3 (which in fact merely incorporates existing gaps and thus is in line with option 2) this option would substantially enlarge access to justice and thus potentially create additional costs, at least for those Member States that especially do not have the far reaching objection procedure (Art 6) and procedure to recognise entities which aim to protect the environment (Art 8) yet;
- Environmental effects would be similar to option 3.

4.4.5 Summary

Table 4.1 below summarises the effects of the four options for the different groups of stakeholders we identified.

Already at the end of the previous section (4.4) we not only looked at the effects of the four options on the behaviour of the stakeholders involved; we equally addressed to what extent the four options could create a level playing field. Of course the question can be asked to what extent creating such a level playing field is a value that should be achieved. This is precisely the issue that will be addressed, from an economic perspective, in the next section.

Table 4.1 Four Options from an Economic Perspective

Stakeholders	Option 1	Option 2	Option 3	Option 4
1. Plaintiffs a. individuals b. NGOs	No legal certainty. NGOs may help create precedents, but uncertainty.	Legal certainty can improve. Uncertainties remain, less (national) suits than optimal.	More legal certainty. Number of suits by NGOs closer to optimal number.	Same as in Option 3. Danger of strategic behaviour by plaintiffs.
2. Defendants	Net cost of trial not to be estimated.	Uncertainties are undesirable.	Defendants will internalise externality; strategic behaviour reduced.	Risk of overdeterrence.
3. Institutions	Relatively low.	Costs of procedures: MSs and Commission.	Costs of implementing directive.	Costs similar to option 3. Also: new preliminary references?
4. Courts	Costs of new preliminary references and uncertainties.	Increasing costs for CJEU and Member States.	Less suits resulting from increased legal certainty. However: more suits because of standing NGOs?	More suits because of standing NGOs? If so: increased workload.
5. Level playing field?	No level playing field; existing differences remain.	Uncertainties remain; no level playing field.	Level playing field more likely than 1 or 2, less uncertainty. More flexible and effective.	Level playing field more likely than 1 or 2, less uncertainty. Cross-border NGO standing not regulated.

4.5 LEVELLING THE PLAYING FIELD

As mentioned above, an important argument in the debate relates to the fact that the lack of a directive completely regulating access to justice in environmental matters may keep existing differences between Member States and thus endanger the creation of a level playing field. It is an argument often advanced by industrial operators and pushed forward to justify harmonisation of environmental law. In this study, focusing on an economic perspective to access to justice this, economically sounding argument of the "need to level the playing field" hence also needs to be addressed. Theoretically, the argument fits into the so-called "pollution haven hypothesis" which will be explained (4.5.1). The important question is especially to what extent empirical evidence exists of such a pollution haven hypothesis (which would hence justify a harmonisation because of a lack of a level playing field) (4.5.2). The crucial question of course remains to what extent differences with respect to access to justice in environmental matters may be of such a nature that they warrant a harmonisation because of the need to "level the playing field" (4.5.3).

4.5.1 *The Pollution Haven Hypothesis*[161]

The race to the bottom holds that in their competition for jobs and tax revenues, jurisdictions will set inefficiently weak environmental standards. Weak environmental standards could take different forms. Either authorities would not set optimal (too lenient) standards or existing standards would not be optimally enforced. Lacking access to justice may also limit a control on (standard setting and enforcement) authorities, as a result of which the suboptimal standard setting would not be remedied. As Levinson explains,[162] the race to the bottom is basically a version of Oates' classic argument as to why redistributive taxes are impossible at the local level.[163] If a local jurisdiction were to impose a Pigouvian tax[164] equal to the local harm from pollution on polluters so as to reduce pollution and provide the local public good of better local environmental quality, the attempt would fail, as the taxing jurisdiction would succeed only in inducing the polluters to move to a jurisdiction that did not tax away their income. The idea is that jurisdictions would engage in a race-to-the-bottom to attract foreign investments. As a result of this,

161 This section of the study is an extension of Faure & Johnston 2009.
162 Levinson 2003, p. 91 and p. 93.
163 Oates 1972.
164 A Pigouvian tax (named after the economist Arthur Pigou) is a tax that is set equal to the amount of external costs caused by *e.g.* a polluter. In this way, the social costs of a negative externality such as pollution will be taken into account by the polluter in his cost-benefit calculations.

prisoners' dilemmas[165] could arise, whereby countries would fail to enact or enforce effective legislation. Jurisdictions are thus supposed to compete against each other with lenient environmental legislation to attract industry.[166] The result would be an overall reduction of environmental quality below efficient levels. This would correspond with the traditional game theoretical result that prisoners' dilemmas create inefficiencies.

Subsequent work has shown that the race to the bottom is in fact not a necessary result, but that there are conditions under which local environmental regulation will provide the efficient level of pollution control. Oates and Schwab[167] showed that if: a) all of the citizens of a jurisdiction work in the polluting industry; b) each suffers equally from pollution; c) labour is fixed in the jurisdiction; d) capital is perfectly mobile but also competitively supplied; and, finally, e) local governments choose the environmental policies that maximise the utility of the median voter, then local pollution taxes will be socially optimal. Essentially, each citizen bears both the full cost and also the full benefit of reducing pollution, and hence chooses the optimal reduction in pollution. But Oates and Schwab's result is not robust with respect to variations in their underlying assumptions. If a local public good must be financed with the pollution tax on mobile capital, then the local pollution tax will be too low, so as to attract capital to essentially pay for the non-environmental public good. If some citizens work in the polluting industry but others collect income from another sources, environmental regulations will be overly lax if the median voter works in the polluting industry, while they will be too strict if the median voter does not work in the polluting industry. Finally, local governments may quite obviously pursue goals other than maximising the aggregate utility of their citizens.[168]

By varying the assumptions underlying the model of decentralised environmental regulatory competition, one can indeed generate anything from a race to the bottom – where local pollution regulations are too weak – to a race to the top – where local pollution regulations are too stringent.[169] Such a race to the top could also lead to overregulation at local level which could equally create inefficiencies.[170] It has especially been David Vogel who has argued that a race to the top could occur in environmental legislation as well. This would be the result of coalitions between environmental NGOs (favouring stringent environmental protection for ecological reasons) and industry groups in highly regulated countries (favouring stringent regulation to create barriers to entry).[171] Ogus argues that

---

165 The prisoner's dilemma is a famous example from game theory, characterised by a noncooperative outcome, whereas the players would have been better off by choosing a cooperative strategy. The players can be different EU Member States, trying to attract industry by lowering environmental standards. If everybody does so, in the end nobody gains (*i.e.* the noncooperative outcome).

166 See Revesz 1992.

167 Oates & Schwab 1988, p. 333.

168 Levinson 2003, pp. 93-94.

169 Wilson 1996; Markusen, Morey & Olewiler 1995, p. 55. See generally Wellisch 2000.

170 See Revesz 1997a, p. 1337; Revesz 1997b, pp. 536-540.

171 Vogel 1995. See also Vogel 2004.

firms may benefit from being located in a high standard jurisdiction since this may generate technological improvements and thus competitive advantages; that may also explain a race-to-the-top.[172]

This theoretical ambiguity is somewhat unsatisfactory. The race-to-the-bottom has been an important argument used to justify federal environmental legislation both in the US and in Europe.[173] Legal scholars continue to debate whether the race to the bottom rationale justifies environmental regulatory federalisation, with law and economics scholars tending to stress the benefits of competition between states or localities,[174] while other legal scholars continue tend to believe in the validity of the race-for-the-bottom rationale for centralisation.[175] They also point in this context at the risk of a so-called 'regulatory chill', meaning that even if countries would not race to the bottom some country may decide not to introduce stringent environmental regulation which it otherwise would for fear that industry might otherwise move to a neighbouring pollution haven. Given the potential significance of the race to the bottom as a rationale for environmental regulatory centralisation and as a normative guide for when such centralisation is economically desirable, the theoretical ambiguity suggests looking to the empirical evidence on whether or not local, sub-national governments can indeed attract industry by setting lenient environmental standards.

4.5.2 *Empirical Evidence*

The empirical evidence on the race to the bottom is inconclusive.[176] Jaffe *et al.* summarised the empirical literature as finding only that that the effects of environmental regulations are "either small, statistically insignificant or not robust to tests of model specification".[177] In their review, Jaffe *et al.* suggested that the stringency of environmental regulations might have some effect on new firms in their decision to locate for the first time,[178] but would not induce existing firms to relocate.[179] They pointed out that other criteria such as tax levels, public services and the unionisation of the labour force have a much more significant impact on the location decision than environmental regulation. Also many

172 Ogus 1999; Van den Bergh, Faure & Lefevere 1996, pp. 141-142.

173 The argument was expressly raised by federal legislators during debate over the American Clean Air and Clean Water Acts, for example. See List & Gerking 2000, p. 453.

174 Revesz 1992, p. 1210; Revesz 1996, p. 2341; Revesz 2000, pp. 37-79.

175 Esty & Geradin 1997; Esty & Geradin 1998.

176 For an overview of the early empirical evidence see Engel 1997, pp. 315-350, who argues that the empirical evidence shows a race-to-the-bottom, which is, however, denied by Revesz 1997.

177 Jaffe, Peterson, Portney & Stavins 1995, pp. 157-158.

178 See Esty & Geradin 1998, pp. 12-15.

179 See on the importance of distinguishing first location decisions from relocation decision List, McHone & Millimet 2003.

other studies have shown that pollution control costs are not major determinants of relocation[180] and that there is little evidence of a pollution haven hypothesis. After all, if this pollution have hypothesis were correct one would have to see decreasing environmental quality in developing countries whereas to the contrary, major urban areas in China, Brazil and Mexico have all experienced significant improvements in air quality.[181] That is not to say that there is no environmental problem in developing countries; the point is simply that empirical research indicates that, with increasing levels of wealth, also in developing countries pollution levels decrease.[182]

Many economists remained somewhat sceptical of the empirical finding that environmental regulations were not a major determinant of industrial location,[183] and more recent empirical work shows that there is indeed an inverse relationship between the stringency of air quality regulations and the level of capital flows in pollution intensive industries.[184] The U.S. Clean Air Act distinguishes between relatively pristine 'attainment' areas and more heavily polluted non-attainment areas by imposing more stringent pollution standards on areas in non-attainment. Research found that even controlling for other observable factors that might influence capital movements, industrial plant growth is significantly higher in less stringently regulated attainment areas than in non-attainment areas. Recent work (which allows for the fact that attainment status is endogenous with respect to plant location decisions, and carefully compares places that are similar in all respects except attainment status), finds an estimated cost to an area of being out of attainment with federal standards of between 0.7 and 1.3 new plants per year, a large percentage loss given that the average county in the sample studied gets only 0.4 new plants per year.[185] List, McHone and Millimet have also examined the effects of air quality regulation on the destination choice of relocating plants. Also that recent study shows that more stringent (air) pollution regulations play a critical role in the siting decision of relocating plants. Their results "provide strong evidence that air quality regulations matter".[186]
Levinson, however, argues that notwithstanding large differences between states in hazardous waste disposal taxes there has not been any pollution haven effect. He provides a variety of explanations, the most important one being that these state hazardous waste disposal taxes do not impose large employment losses on industries that generate waste.[187]

180 For a summary, see Dasgupta *et al.* 2002, pp. 159-160.
181 Dasgupta *et al.* 2002, pp. 160-162.
182 For a summary of this literature see Faure 2012, pp. 297-299.
183 *E.g.*, Xing & Kolstad 1995, argued that the laxity of environmental regulations in a host country is a significant determinant of foreign direct investment by the US chemical industry.
184 Becker & Henderson 2000; Greenstone 2002, p. 1175.
185 List, Millimet, Fredriksson & McHone 2003, p. 948.
186 List, McHone & Millimet 2003, p. 658.
187 Levinson 2000.

Other recent empirical work has tackled the problem of controlling for the full range of variables (besides just environmental regulatory stringency) that affect firm locational choice. Working with a more detailed dataset and again employing a propensity score matching estimator, Millimet and List[188] found that even at the very local (U.S. county) level, location-specific attributes such as unemployment levels and the overall level of manufacturing employment significantly impact the effect of environmental regulatory stringency. Millimet and List found that the cost of strict environmental regulations is lower both for counties with high unemployment – because they have relatively abundant, cheap labour – as well as for counties with a greater concentration of employment in manufacturing – because such counties generate agglomeration economies for manufacturing firms.

In sum, the new empirical literature on the 'race-to-the-bottom' has found that environmental regulations have statistically significant, large effects on industrial location,[189] effects that were previously either missed entirely or seriously underestimated.[190] However, it should be stressed that most of this empirical research focuses on competition between American states; the situation may be different in Europe where there is less evidence (at least as the old member states are concerned) of a 'race-to-the-bottom'.

As far as whether state environmental regulators are acting strategically, taking account of regulatory stringency in states with which they compete for capital and hence jobs, empirical research has found a positive relationship between environmental regulatory stringency (measured by normalised environmental abatement costs) in competitor states.[191] A recent study also finds a similarly strong positive relationship between the environmental enforcement efforts of competitor states, with a 10% increase in a competitor state's enforcement efforts leading to between a 5 and 16% increase in the own state's enforcement efforts.[192]

Summarising, earlier empirical studies indicated that given high relocation costs firms will not relocate to a pollution haven also because costs of pollution abatement are only a relatively small portion of total production costs. More recent empirical evidence from the US, however, sheds a somewhat different light and shows that differences in pollution

---

188 Millimet & List 2004, p. 239.

189 Levinson 2003, p. 96.

190 Results of a meta-analysis of literally hundreds of studies by Jeppesen, List & Folmer 2002, 21 show that the odd earlier results showing that the locational decisions of polluting and non-polluting industries were similarly influenced by environmental regulations may have been due to the failure of earlier studies to control for variables such as factor composition and mobility and lobbying power.

191 Fredriksson & Millimet 2002, p. 101; this finding in Fredriksson and Millimet was replicated by Levinson 2003.

192 Konisky 2008. Research by Gray & Shadbegian 2007 also found that the number of inspections at a plant, at nearby plants and at plants in the same state were associated with greater compliance, but that inspections at nearby plants in other states did not seem to increase compliance. This also seems to confirm a competition between states as far as enforcement activity is concerned.

abatement costs between states may be substantial. Moreover, even though relocation to a pollution haven may not be realistic, pollution control costs could influence the *ex ante* decision of industry on choosing an appropriate location. Finally, literature has also indicated that relaxing environmental enforcement efforts in one state could lead neighbouring, competing, states to reduce enforcement efforts as well.[193] Hence, differences between Member States law (and hence a lacking level playing field) may be problematic even when they will not lead to a relocation of firms to a 'pollution haven'; a competition via weak enforcement could from that perspective be equally problematic.

4.5.3 *Applied to Access to Justice*

There have been a few interesting studies within the EU on the effects of environmental policy on European business and its competitiveness. More particularly a commission staff working document of 2004[194] applies the economic notion of competitiveness to environmental policy and pays specific attention to the single market aspects of environmental policy. The document rightly holds:

> Having rules and legislation at EU level ensures a level playing field for companies operating in the Single Market[195]

And:

> In addition, national measures to protect the environment can contribute, directly or indirectly, to making the free movement of goods more difficult and expensive. [...] This is why it would be important from a competitiveness point of view that environmental policy encourages the full respect of the Single Market.[196]

The study concludes:

> All in all, differences in stringency of environmental regulations between the EU and third countries, whether justified for the above reasons or not, could have an impact on price competitiveness of European producers, which in some cases could be significant.[197]

193 This effect is sometimes referred to as a 'regulatory chill'. See Esty & Geradin 1997 and Esty & Geradin 1998.
194 SEC(2004) 769 of 10 June 2004.
195 SEC(2004) 769, p. 9.
196 SEC(2004) 769, p. 10.
197 SEC(2004) 769, p. 11.

Even though this study mainly addresses the competitiveness of European producers *vis-à-vis* producers in third countries (especially addressing the worry that European environmental law would make European products or services too costly) the study is interesting since it raises the point, also addressed in the pollution haven literature, being that differences in stringency of environmental regulation can create substantial price differences. The extent to which this is the case has been addressed *inter alia* in an interesting study for the European Commission by De Sadeleer and others.[198] They examined access to justice in environmental matters in eight Member States and also presented some empirical findings on access to justice. One important result was that the actual number of court cases brought by environmental NGOs in the various Member States differs widely from *e.g.* 4 in Denmark to 4,000 in the Netherlands[199] in the period between 1996 and 2001. These authors notice not only that the legal rules concerning access to the courts in environmental matters differ broadly between the Member States, but also that the actual number of cases differs. They conclude that there are "wide empirical disparities between Member States with regard to access to justice in environmental matters by environmental NGOs".[200] Interestingly though, the same study also concludes that the cases brought by environmental associations are relatively more successful than the average law suit. They conclude:

> The high success rate of actions brought by environmental associations in the public interest also indicates that they fulfil an important function in the enforcement of environmental law and that they are generally brought for legally sound reasons.[201]

Another interesting conclusion of the study is that NGO actions play an increasing role in environmental law but are still few in number compared to the overall number of law suits. This is also the case in which broad access to justice is allowed. The study concludes:

> Compared to the overall number of actions brought before the courts in the Member States studied, the relative figure itself is low, and sometimes even at a level that is insignificant. This study does clearly refuse the argument that environmental public interest actions lead to an overload in the courts.[202]

This hence seems to be an important conclusion in the framework of this study since apparently even in Member States with broad access to justice the number of law suits

198 De Sadeleer, Roller & Dross 2002.
199 *Ibid.*, p. 3.
200 *Ibid.*, p. 5.
201 *Ibid.*, p. 8.
202 *Ibid.*, p. 33.

remains low and does not lead to an overload in the courts. This study would hence support the argument that the marginal costs of moving from a status quo to *e.g.* option 3 discussed above would not be substantial. On the other hand, the study also indicated that substantial differences still may exist between Member States as a result of which costs of private operators may differ as well. The extent to which differences in access to justice in environmental matters lead to differences that should be considered that important that they may lead to a pollution haven or a regulatory chill obviously needs further empirical examination in the country studies.

4.6 Preliminary Conclusions

This chapter, providing an economic approach to access to justice in environmental matters, *inter alia* sketched the basic economic arguments for a standing requirement in civil procedure, explaining at the same time that in environmental matters a so-called 'rational apathy' or rational disinterest may occur which may precisely justify a broadening of standing in those matters, because otherwise environmental externalities may not be sufficiently internalised. We also provided an analysis of the incentives of the various stakeholder groups in the procedure related to access to justice, focusing on potential plaintiffs and defendants, administrations and institutions, and the judiciary (courts). This stakeholder analysis was important to allow us to proceed to an analysis of the four options for further action at EU level with respect to access to justice in environmental matters.

We argued that although all options lead to specific costs and benefits, the first two options have the disadvantage that legal uncertainty (and related social and private costs) will remain substantial since the effects of these options to a large extent depend upon Member State law and (with respect to option 2) the outcomes of infringement procedures. Options 3 and 4 both rely on the creation of a new directive which has the advantage that these uncertainty costs would be reduced. Options 3 and 4 also both have common benefits for stakeholders (like enterprises and NGOs), namely that procedures would be harmonised, procedural guarantees would be included and legal certainty would be created. Access to justice would be substantially enlarged in both options, especially in option 4, where it may even lead to over-deterrence and where also new legal questions may arise as a result of the broad scope of proposal COM(2003) 624. Option 3 on the other hand would also have the possibility of creating an optional environmental mediation into a new proposal. This may at this stage lead to a slight preference for option 3.

However, the extent to which a particular option is preferred also depends on existing differences in Member State law and on the question whether these differences may negatively affect the internal market. That question was first theoretically analysed by addressing the so-called pollution haven hypothesis that makes clear that differences in stringency of environmental regulation (and obviously also of enforcement via access to justice) may have an influence on industry (re)location. It fits within the game theoretical notion of the race-to-the-bottom explaining that Member States would compete to attract industry with a favourable environmental provisions (hence potentially with less attractive access to justice in environmental matters). Although largely of American origin, empirical studies of a more recent date seem to provide some support for this pollution haven hypothesis. At least differences in environmental stringency, but also in enforcement, seem to be statistically significant.

Of course, the question arises to what extent differences between Member States as far as access to justice in environmental matters are concerned are that significant that they could endanger the level playing field and would hence warrant harmonisation. This is indeed one of the questions that will be dealt with in the country studies, to be introduced briefly in Chapter 6 of this book.

5 Environmental Democracy and Access to Justice: A Comparative Law and Society Approach

Leïla Choukroune and Michael Faure

5.1 Environmental PIL as a Recent Phenomenon in Europe

As emphasised by the UNECE Access to Justice Task Force itself,[1] the justiciability of the right to the environment as a socio-economic right cannot be achieved without taking into consideration the main actors of the whole process in a broader societal context. If engaging in the elaboration of a new proposal (*i.e.* options 3 and 4), the Commission would indeed have to address the socio-legal specificities and the potential societal impact of its work in rather diverse European socio-legal systems.

While the European Court of Human Rights (ECtHR) has referred to the Aarhus Convention in a number of recent decisions,[2] the ECtHR approach to standing remains quite narrow and cannot be compared to a PIL process. According to Article 34 of the European Convention on Human Rights (ECHR), every individual, NGO or group of individuals can file a complaint to the ECtHR, provided that this claimant is a victim of a violation by one of the 'High Contracting Parties' of a substantive conventional right. From this legal obligation, one understands that the complainant cannot act as the representative of the public interest and seek remedies for others than himself. Hence *action popularis* is not permitted by the ECHR nor has it been accepted by the ECtHR, as clarified by the Asselbourg decision according to which an NGO "cannot claim to be the victim of an infringement of the right to respect for its 'home' within the meaning of Article 8 of the Convention".[3] For

---

1 See <www.unece.org/env/pp/a.to.j.html>.

2 The Aarhus Convention was quoted, *e.g.*, in ECtHR, *Tatar v. Romania*, 67021/01, 29 January 2009, and mentioned in ECtHR, *Branduse v. Romania*, 6586/03, 7 April 2009. For other cases before the ECHR that concern issues covered by the Aarhus Convention, see, *e.g.*, ECtHR, *Zander v. Sweden*, 45/1992/390/468 of 25 October 1993; ECtHR, *Guerra et al. v. Italy*, 14967/89 of 19 February 1998.; ECtHR, *Taskin et al. v. Turkey*, 46117/99 of 10 November 2004); ECtHR, *Giacomelli v. Italy*, 59909/00, 2 November 2006; ECtHR, *Okyay et al. v. Turkey*, 36220/97 of 12 July 2005; ECtHR, *Társaság a Szabadságjogokért v. Hungary*, 37374/05, 14 April 2009; ECtHR, *Kenedi v. Hungary*, Application 31475/05, 26 May 2009.

3 See *Asselbourg and 78 Others and Greenpeace Luxemburg v. Luxemburg* (Appl. No. 29121/95) ECtHR, 29 June 1999.

these reasons the current European supranational judicial system has not been very PIL friendly.

Moreover, before the entry into force of the Aarhus Convention, the vast majority of European legal systems only allowed the 'victim' or the 'aggrieved party' to seek a remedy for the environmental wrong he/she suffered from. The absence of a direct link to environmental damages precluded access to judicial remedies. This was without considering the impact these environmental cases had on the 'public' at large and the possibility for non-aggrieved parties to act *as if* they were directly impacted and *on behalf* of the 'public interest' of a given country or even a broader community of countries in the precise case of the EU. The European Commission itself recognised that private parties were not the main drivers of environmental law enforcement while this needed implementation was often referred to as 'public concern' going far beyond the traditional legal boundaries between private and public interests.[4] This irruption of the 'public' in the European legal debate through the intervention of UNECE was not and is still not always welcome in European legal systems (either at the national levels or at the EU level itself)[5] that have not until very recently developed public interest lawyering and litigation practices.

To better gauge the possible impact and limitations of the development of this nascent European environmental PIL, one needs first to confront this relatively new phenomenon with preexisting foreign comparable trends in paying a special attention to the issue of standing and more precisely the many conceptions developed on the *locus standi* theory in countries where environmental PIL has reached a certain level of sophistication and is now sometimes rejected as a costly, not well suited and ineffective avenue to reach a greater environmental justice. This combination of legal techniques and doctrines helps us better gauge the desirability of an increased access to justice, the bottom line being (and this of course corresponds with the economic perspective developed in the previous chapter) that one may not always assume that a larger access automatically leads to greater environmental justice.

For these reasons, and in addition to the Law and Economics approach presented in the previous chapter, it is important to address the issue of access to justice for a greater European environmental democracy from a Law and Society angle, in relation to the concepts of PIL and in a comparative manner.

What is a Law and Society angle? While the sociological perspective on law[6] is often contrasted with the analytical perspective, our approach proposes to reconcile these different theoretical schools of thought, hence clearly linking the Law and Society analysis to the

4 European Commission, *Implementing Community Environmental Law*, COM 96, 500 (final), 22 October 1996.
5 See Poncelet 2012.
6 Pound 1911.

Law and Economics framework presented above. Beyond the generally accepted aphorism according to which "law is a social phenomenon", we use positive law to look at its social implications, effects or causes in a comparative manner. To do so in respecting the space limitation of this study, we have chosen to focus on the foreign roots and previous experiences of Public Interest Environmental Litigation as well as on the many institutions and actors, which have played and are playing a role in the access to justice debate in the selected countries examples.

5.2 The Indian Roots of PIL

PIL emerged as a rights advocacy strategy in the United States civil rights movement of the 1960s and has been broadly used worldwide to describe the many ways general grievances relating to the enforcement of socio-economic rights have been litigated by the courts and remedies awarded to the victims of the State. But 'Public Interest Litigation' as well as 'Public Interest Lawyering' are too often used as catch-all phrases covering quite different manifestations, from the legal aid services offered to the poorest to all types of procedures used in either public or private law to redress specific or general wrongs, hence advancing broader socio-political objectives. However, it is probably in Asia, and precisely in India, that PIL has achieved its most sophisticated, yet sometimes ambiguous variation.[7] As convincingly demonstrated by Upendra Baxi in a landmark article published in 1985, that is a few years after the end of the 1975-1976 Emergency period and at a time "judicial democracy" was revolutionising Indian politics, the "extraordinary remedies" the Indian population was seeking out differed from the PIL general significance. They were indeed "transcending the received notions of separation of powers and the inherited distinctions between adjudication and legislation on the one hand and administration and adjudication on the other". Not to mention that they brought "*a new kind of lawyering and a novel kind of judging*".[8] Oriented towards the 'rural poor' and not, as it had progressively been the case in the US, in the direction of civic participation in governmental decision making and eventually the representation of 'interests without groups'[9], the Indian incarnation of PIL was essentially social. This 'Social Action Litigation' (SAL)[10], as conceived by Uprenda Baxi, was "primarily judge-led and even judge-induced" and as such "elated to juristic and judicial activism on the High Bench".[11] The Indian SAL trend was not deprived of

7 While relatively few publications refer to the PIL terminology when dealing with the United States, a large number of articles and books have been released about Asia (and more specifically, India). See for instance Yap & Lau 2010, Rao 2004, Razzaque 2004 and DasGupta 2009.

8 Baxi 1985, p. 108.

9 *Ibid.*, p. 109.

10 *Ibid.*, p. 108.

11 *Ibid.*, p. 111.

populist rhetoric and judicial politics although putting forward humanist aspirations. But as demonstrated in the seminal decision *Kesavananda Bharati*,[12] these ambitions were also framed by the division of powers and the inherent limitation of constitutional precedent:

> these landmarks in the development of the law cannot be permitted to be transformed into weapons for defeating the hopes and aspirations of our teeming millions, half-clad, half-starved, half-educated. These hopes and aspirations representing the will of the people can only become articulate through the voice of their elected representatives. If they fail the people, the nation must face death and destruction. Then neither the Court nor the Constitution will save the country.[13]

> Whenever there is a public wrong or public injury caused by an act or omission of the State or a public authority which is contrary to the Constitution or the law, any member of the public acting bona fide and having sufficient interest can maintain an action for redressal of such wrong or public injury. (. . .)

> If public duties are to be enforced and social collective 'diffused' rights and interests are to be protected, we have to utilize the initiative and zeal of public minded persons and organizations by allowing them to move the court and act for a general or group interest; even though, they may not be directly injured in their own rights.[14]

Interestingly, the Indian SAL has shifted from the poor to the middle class, hence getting closer to its American predecessor, but also from basic socio-economic rights to more complex issues such as the protection of the environment, thereby providing an excellent Law and Society comparison for our analysis.

The majority of environmental law cases in India since 1985 has indeed been brought before the court as writ petitions, usually by individuals acting on *pro bono* basis. In this context the role of certain NGOs or individuals (from lawyers to self-taught legal activists)

---

12 See *Kesavnanda Bharathi v. State of Kerala* (1973) 4 SCC 225. This landmark decision constitutes the basis for the Indian Supreme Court to review parliamentary constitutional amendments. Dealing essentially with property right, this seminal case is key to Indian constitutional history as it elaborates on the "basis structure" doctrine: while fundamental rights can be amended, the Parliament cannot alter the "basis structure of the constitution". See also Andhyarujina (2011).

13 Justice Chandrachud in Kesavananda at 968, quoted by Baxi 1985, p. 112.

14 See Justice Bhagwati's fascinating reasoning in *S.P. Gupta v. Union of India*, AIR 1982 SC 149: 1981, at 190-194. This case is often contemplated as the precursor of the Indian PIL. PIL writ petitions have been filed under Art 226 (Power of High Courts to issue certain writs) or Art 32 (remedies for enforcement of (fundamental) rights guaranteed by the Constitution) of the Indian Constitution.

has been crucial. This led to major decisions from the Supreme Court. In *Subhash Kumar v. State of Bihar*[15] the Indian Supreme Court recognised the right to the environment as a fundamental right. In another PIL case, *Vellore Citizen Welfare Forum v. Union of India & Ors*, the Supreme Court introduced the precautionary principle in Indian environmental law. Further, in a PIL case filed by M.C. Mehta, *Mehta v. Union of India,*[16] the Indian Supreme Court propounded the absolute liability principle. In each of these cases, the actors involved have played a key role in broadening the locus standi offering a greater access and eventually a better justice for the aggrieved citizens. But the latest developments of the Indian environmental PIL have also been criticised for offering only a forum for judicial political activism and not justice.

PIL hencc is based on the idea that the judiciary should redress failures of the executive to enact and enforce laws in the public interest. The well-known Indian justice Krishna Iyer (one of the proponents of environmental PIL) mentioned in that respect:

> The categorical imperative for stability in democracy is, therefore, to see that every instrumentality is functionally kept on course and any deviants or misconduct, abuse or aberration, corruption or delinquency is duly monitored and disciplinary measures taken promptly to make unprofitable for the delinquents to depart from the code of conduct and to make it possible for people, social activists, professional leaderships and other duly appointed agencies to enforce punitive therapeutics when robed culprits violate moral-legal norms.[17]

5.3 SOME RECENT FOREIGN DEVELOPMENTS OF ENVIRONMENTAL PIL

5.3.1 Access, Participation and Equity and Justice in the Recent Indian Environmental PIL

As briefly explained above, the Indian judge has not only integrated well-established principles of environmental law into Indian environmental jurisprudence, but also a series of nascent concepts (notion of sustainable development[18], precautionary principle[19], idea of the State as a trustee of all natural resources[20]). However, as demonstrated in the quite

15 *Subhash Kumar v. State of Bihar* (1991), 1 SCC 598.
16 *Mehta v. Union of India* (1992), 1 SCC 358.
17 Iyer 1994, p. 265.
18 *Mehta v. Union of India* (1997).
19 *Vellore Citizens' Welfare Forum v. Union of India* (1996).

abundant academic literature on the topic,[21] this evolution did not happen without raising a number of fundamental concerns about access, participation and equity in an judicial system, which was already very much criticised for confusing political and legal objectives. The 'personal' involvement of the judge was indeed key in many of the recent Indian environmental PIL cases. As stated already by Justice Chandrachud in the late 1970s in the landmark decision *State of Rajasthan v. Union of India*: "it is an accepted fact of constitutional interpretation that the content of justiciability changes according to how the Judge's value preferences respond to the multi-dimensional problems of the day".[22] In such a judge-led system it has been inevitable to see a limitation or, on the contrary, broadening of access in relation to the judges personal inclinations. Certain social values or preferences have directly influenced access and participation to the court. As clearly demonstrated by Lavanya Rajamani indeed:

> The perception of the judiciary as middle class intellectuals with middle class preferences for fewer slums, cleaner air and garbage-free streets, at any cost (to others), has in itself silenced certain voices. The poor, and those who represent them, are unlikely to approach the Court with their concerns, as they are likely to be left the poorer for it.[23]

This is rather paradoxical given the origins and history of the Indian PIL or SAL as described by Uprenda Baxi. While the liberalisation of the *locus standi* was indeed initially conceived to address the problem of poorest, the court is now dealing with the Indian middle class' preoccupation with a clean environment. As a result, a number of recent decisions have been viewed as less participatory (reluctance of the judge to give access to certain NGOs representing poor communities) and so not equitable.[24] This might also be explained by the changing and so problematic nature of the tasks performed by the judge who is asked to supplement the inefficient executive in addressing socio-economic questions of very broad nature. The judge does not only interpret the law, but creates it as he did a number of times on the basis of Article 32 of the Indian Constitution (enforcement of a fundamental right).[25] This resulted and is resulting today in a disaffection if

20 *M.C. Mehta v. Kamal Nath* 1997.

21 See for instance Rajamani 2007.

22 See *State of Rajasthan v. Union of India* (1977), 3 SCC 592, 648.

23 Rajamani 2007, p. 303.

24 *M.C. Metha v. Union of India* (Delhi Vehicular Pollution Case (1998)). For a very interesting account of the major environmental cases, see MC Mehta Environmental Foundation, available at: <http://mcmef.org/landmark_cases.html/>.

25 See *Vishaka v. State of Rajasthan* (1997). In this PIL case, the judge has supplemented the legislator in producing guidelines defining sexual harassment in the workplace and providing for a whole set of procedural rules for investigation and remedy.

not reluctance against PIL and environmental PIL in particular. Public Interest Litigation is often said to transform into personal interest litigation or frivolous and often political interest litigation.

5.3.2 *Environmental PIL with Chinese Characteristics*

Another fascinating example of the development, utilisation and limitations of environmental Public Interest Litigation is provided by the recent evolutions of Chinese case law. A unique incarnation of Public Interest Litigation is indeed progressively appearing in China. Referring to general grievances litigated in relation to the implementation of social and economic rights, the Chinese nascent approach of PIL is not judge-led nor is it judge-induced as in the Indian case. In an authoritarian one party state,[26] the inexistence of a truly independent and professional judiciary could of course partly explain this key difference, but other Chinese specificities come into play.[27] For the past five to ten years indeed, China law scholars and China watchers have been observing the birth, development, and logical limitations of a rights-based and civil society-led movement using the law as well as existing judicial avenues as powerful tools for social emancipation, hence furthering the basic legal regime offered by the Chinese Constitution and other legislative developments. Interestingly, this sinicisation of PIL finds its roots and strength in the use of rights-based tools themselves powerfully reinforced by a language of rights largely disseminated by the media – including official channels – and ambiguously tolerated by a state that both generates and limits rights. While a number of rights are concerned by this grassroots-led movement, it is in the labour law field as well as in environmental law that China is developing its most interesting and, as we will see, most debatable if not controversial variation of PIL.

Since the 2004 amendments, the Chinese Constitution recognises 'private property' and stressed the state's intention to "respect and protect human rights". This language of rights has penetrated the Chinese population from the Supreme People's Court to the Chinese workers and citizens who are now referring to the Constitution as an instrument for protection and development of their socio-economic rights. In parallel to these constitutional changes, China started to develop its environmental law from the end of 1970s when the need to address the first environmental issues arising from economic development became more obvious. Some Chinese scholars estimate that 10% of the new legislation

26 A number of authors have interrogated the politics and practices of courts in authoritarian regimes. See Ginsburg & Tamir 2008.

27 In their work on PIL in Asia, Po Jen Yap and Holing Lau identify three main engines for the development of PIL: "democratization, transnational migration of norms and ideals, judicial recognition of the institutional role of courts in shaping public law discourse within their jurisdiction". See Yap & Lau (2011).

adopted in China during the past 30 years deal with environmental questions. But many of these 'green laws' are also perceived as useless by the same scholars.[28] Indeed, these many norms suffer from a dramatic absence of implementation that has resulted in a fantastic surge in environmental disputes. The number of disputes on pollution seems to have increased by 25% per year since 1996. There are 86 specialised environmental courts in China established in 14 provinces that is about half of the Chinese provinces.[29] These specialised courts play a leading role in broadening the standing as they accept technical cases the regular courts would not have accepted. Although environmental Public Interest Litigation is not expressly permitted in Chinese civil procedural law (a direct interest must indeed exist for a plaintiff to bring a lawsuit[30]), it has received the recent support of the Chinese government. As for labour Public Interest Litigation, the government's choice to support this new type of litigation is relatively easy to understand: the cases brought to court are relatively technical and do not directly question the government political choices. Court centric, the Chinese environmental Public Interest Litigation believes in the capacity of the current judicial system to enforce the rights claimed by the Chinese population. Oriented towards the working class and not only the poorest strata of the society, it indeed tends to focus on wider interests, hence participating in the protection of all citizens' rights.

This new 'green court' movement has not blossomed completely by chance. As we have seen, it has been supported by the legislative reform and the government itself and is also the result of long-term training programmes and awareness raising campaigns often organised by foreign donors. Not only the legal professionals were better informed and trained, but a number of powerful NGOs developed throughout the whole Chinese territory. These NGOs as well as specialised law firms help the aggrieved citizens bring their case to the Chinese courts. Lastly, the Environmental Protection Bureaux (EPB), specialised agencies generally affiliated to a Municipal government also played a key role in bringing new suits.

In the *All China Environment Federation and Guiyang Public Environment Education Centre v. Dingpa Paper Mill of Wudang District City*,[31] the All China Environment Federation (ACEF), together with Guiyang Public Environmental Education Centre, brought a Public Interest Litigation case in Qingzhen Environmental Court requesting a Company, Dingap Paper Mill, to stop discharging industrial waste water in the Nanming River what caused dangerous water pollution. The court recognised that the two plaintiffs, as lawfully registered environmental protection organisations can represent the public interest and

28 See the work of Prof. Wang Jin from Peking University and the "China Dialogues", available at: <www.chinadialogue.net/article/show/single/en/3831--China-s-green-laws-are-useless->.

29 Zhang & Zhang 2012.

30 Art 108 of the Civil Procedure Law of the People's Republic of China.

31 See Verdict n°4, Civil Environment Cases of the Qingzhen First Instance People's Court (2010).

eventually ruled in favour of the plaintiffs. It is actually the first successful environmental public interest case brought by an 'NGO' in China. But those who know China would have already understood that this type of 'NGO' is not exactly close to what western NGOs are about. The ACEF is supported and managed by a number of former or current government officials and so legitimated by Beijing itself. The same ACEF supported by the United Nations Development Programme (UNDP) has recently won an "information disclosure and transparency related" case. The case had to do with the failure of a local environment protection bureau in the Xiuwen county to release information requested by the ACEF in relation to the Guizhou Haoyiduo Dietary Company including its waste water discharge permit and other waste management related documents. The case was open to the public, ruled in favour of ACEF and is now showcased as an example of promoting freedom of information and even judicial review via the intervention of civil society organs.[32]

But these ambiguities in the NGOs status are also used to bring procedural changes and have contributed to the broadening of the standing for environmental cases. These procedural innovations occur at the local level with the direct or implicit support of the local governments. The Guiyang intermediate People's Court, for instance, issued a series of documents and orders to establish rules on how to hand cases in the Guiyang and Qinzhen environmental courts. According to these quite uncommon rules, procuratorates, administrative and specialised agencies as well as environmental NGOs have standing to bring an environmental Public Interest Litigation. Similar local rules were adopted in Wuxi and in Yunnan although the later province seems reluctant to implement these rules and accept environmental Public Interest Litigations.[33]

The Chinese environmental Public Interest Litigation is one fascinating illustration of this ability to adapt and perpetuate a given system. In this context one needs to question the possible side effects of 'justiciability' and broader access to justice in an authoritarian state such as China. Far from challenging the regime, a manifestation of justiciability such as the Chinese environmental PIL can also reinforce the existing political system in providing the leaders with breathing time and space. While there is more access to courts, there is not necessarily more justice and more environmental democracy.

5.3.3 *South Africa: The Need to Challenge the Legal Culture*

The South African situation brings another very interesting comparative example of the relative failure of environmental Public Interest Litigation while the new legal context

32 See UNDP China, available at: <www.undp.org.cn/modules.php?op=modload&name=News&file=article&catid=14&topic=33&sid=44748&mode=nocomments&order=0&thold=0>.

33 Wand & Gao (2010).

(Bill of Rights and National Environmental Management Act) had considerably increased opportunities for environmental PIL. In the landmark case of *Director: Mineral Development, Gauteng Region v. State the Vaal Environment*,[34] the South African Court made the following observation:

> Our Constitution by including environmental rights as fundamental, justiciable human rights, by necessary implication requires that environmental considerations be accorded appropriate recognition and respect in the administrative processes in our country. Together with the change in the ideological climate must also come a change in our legal and administrative approach to environmental concerns.

However, observers generally agree on the very limited utilisation of the legislative possibilities offered in the post-apartheid area for environmental litigation. In a number of recent cases indeed, the South African courts have been very strict in interpreting, for instance, the personal interest requirement for *locus standi*. One of the reasons scholars generally put forward to explain the reluctance of the judiciary to broaden the access to the court for environmental violations relates to the absence of an appropriate legal culture and the need for additional time for the legislative changes to permeate the minds of the judiciary and the lawyers.[35]

5.4 Limits of PIL

As demonstrated above the expansion of the *locus standi* does not necessarily bring more environmental justice nor greater environmental democracy. Giving 'public spirited' citizens the right to move courts can also have negative effects (cf. the side effects of option 4 on NGOs and other civil society stakeholders identified in the table in Section 4.4.5 above).[36] First, it is not clear yet in Europe that there would be a substantial number of citizens who would choose to move the courts on behalf of an affected community. That is, a rational choice theory does not explain why a citizen would do so. The same arguments that apply to the undersupply of public goods, apply here as well. If, however, there is a private gain to the person or persons who initiate Public Interest Litigation, it becomes imperative to know what these gains are. The danger remains that PIL may be used to

34 See *Director: Mineral Development, Gauteng Region v. State the Vaal Environment*, 1999 2 SA 709 (SCA), para. 20.

35 Kidd 2010.

36 See in this respect especially Cha 2005, who holds that an expended doctrine of *locus standi* may end up harming, not helping the judicial process.

serve private interests. In such a case, the judge has to decide whether to admit the case or not. If a large number of cases were to be filed, this would prove to be an extra cost to the judiciary.[37] These costs must be weighed against the litigation's potential benefits, both the *ex post* as well as *ex ante* deterrence that it can create.

5.5 Outlook

Having in mind the differences in contexts and legal history and cultures, these comparative elements nevertheless provide some insight into why a requirement of *locus standi* may be necessary but why, more particularly in environmental cases, relaxing *locus standi* is important from an economic perspective as well as long as the benefits of such a relaxation exceed the costs. The basic notion that sticking to a very strict standing requirement and restricting access to justice may in environmental cases not be in the public interest is a very crucial notion for the case of access to justice in Europe as well.

In this regard, these comparative studies also help us test our four options from a different perspective. Indeed, they show that option 1 is probably not desirable as it would only comfort the existing situation without addressing the gaps in Member States' legislation. In countries where environmental PIL has developed and brought key results, there was not only a political will, but also the adoption of clear – although often minimal – legal reforms. A similar remark could be formulated with regards to the second option studied. While it would help disseminate the current ECJ case law and *de facto* contribute to a greater awareness of the problems they address, it would not bring the legal certainty and harmonisation expected to clarify a rather complex, *i.e.* extremely diverse legal environment. These changes, however, need to be put in place in a relatively consensual manner, that is, gathering the support of all stakeholders at all levels of the institutional edifice. In this regard, option 4 seems to be less realistic as there might still be some opposition to the Commission's original proposal. The third option then appears as the best compromise between the need to better implement ECJ case law and EC previous directives while preserving the regulatory autonomy of Member States. From the comparative studies briefly addressed above, one also learns that any option chosen should be accompanied by other adequate measures that would help develop a genuine legal culture in favour of environmental PIL. From lawyers to judges and civil society organisations or enterprises, this could only be achieved through complementary programs of legal education and training themselves helping the implementation of option 3.

37 See Cha 2005, p. 210, who holds that liberalisation of standing can result in a flood of litigation (delaying trials), may lead to an abuse of the liberal standing for personal gains and to a loss of the legitimacy by the courts.

Indeed, our brief comparative studies have shown how important judicial and non-judicial actors are in bringing – or not – more environmental justice. Without a different legal culture, legislative innovations will not help achieve the expected results in countries that do not share the same approach to the role of the state and the judiciary. A greater access to justice will not necessarily lead to a better implementation of the existing environmental rules if there is nothing done additionally in terms of awareness raising and training of judges, lawyers, NGOs and business. In this regard, the different pillars of the Aarhus Convention if applied cumulatively will participate to the improvement of environmental justice situation.

6 Empirical Survey: Country Studies

Fokke Fernhout, Niels Philipsen and Leïla Choukroune

6.1 Goal of the Survey

In the empirical part of this research, the conclusions (hypotheses) of our Law and Economics analysis and our Law and Society analysis will be confronted with the opinions of those actually involved in access to justice in environmental cases. We supplement the theoretical analysis by examining how the access to justice implications of the various options are perceived by lawyers who are directly experiencing the workings of access to justice in their everyday work. From these impressions, we will try to derive some useful insights to guide the decision making process regarding the four options.

6.2 Methodology

For several reasons the hypotheses put forward in Chapter 4 cannot be tested by analyzing statistical or empirical data. Firstly, the hypotheses derived from the law and economics literature are not formulated as "social or economic patterns" expressed in quantifiable parameters. Although correlations are well known, it is difficult to predict the actual changes caused by varying one of the parameters. Secondly, in Section 4.4 we already noted that an analysis at this level would require a micro-analysis of each of the Member States, which falls far beyond the scope of this study. Thirdly, the models of law and economics have a tendency to isolate phenomena that can be quantified theoretically. Characteristics of specific populations are not taken into account, whereas in reality these characteristics form an important factor that should not be overlooked when assessing the possible outcome of measures to be taken in the field of access to justice. Lastly, contrary to what we expected, statistical information on environmental cases was not available in any of the countries that have been selected (see Section 6.3 below). Court statistics do exist, but do not specify environmental cases as a specific category.

The research is therefore conducted by means of interviews with lawyers representing different stakeholders. Estimations of future developments are exclusively based on the views of the respondents in relation with the qualitative aspects of the analysis of Chapter 4.

It would be unwise to ask the respondents only to assess the possible developments following one of the four options (already for the simple reason that option 3, the enacting of a new directive, is not precise enough to allow for an assessment of its consequences). Therefore, these options have been broken down into specific elements that could be part of any option. These specific elements are like building blocks that cover the range of issues and choices at the disposition of the Commission to steer environmental access to justice in new directions.

The respondents were selected from the groups of stakeholders identified in Chapter 4 of this report (plaintiffs, operators, administrative authorities, judiciary), although we should note that it turned out to be impossible to find respondents for each stakeholder group for each country. All respondents were lawyers acting on behalf or as member of one or more of the stakeholders. The respondents received a customised questionnaire and list of topics in advance to prepare for the interview (examples are included in Appendices 1-3). The interviews were held by telephone or Skype and lasted approximately one hour. Each interview was summarised in a report, which was submitted for review to the respondent.[1]

Lawyers acting on behalf of plaintiffs were *inter alia* interviewed on the considerations to sue, whereas potential defendants were interviewed on the effects of all elements, including the option of 'leveling the playing field'. In addition, the 'system costs' were addressed, *i.e.* the burden that the various options put on the judiciary system in the Member State concerned. Finally, all stakeholders were asked to comment on the current situation and thus – indirectly – on the costs of inaction (option 1).

6.3 Country Selection

The countries were selected primarily on the basis of information provided in the Darpö study, with the intention to focus on two Member States with wide access to justice and two Member States with restricted access to justice. Of the four countries thus selected only three could be included in the survey, since the fourth country (Portugal) did not respond to requests addressed to potential respondents.

Nevertheless, the three remaining countries offer a useful spectre of initial situations, as these countries are situated on different positions of different scales. When it comes to *standing* rules (or the requirement of 'sufficient interest') especially Latvia (four respondents) and the United Kingdom (four respondents, three from England & Wales and one from Scotland) are extremely liberal, although for Scotland this is a quite recent development. In practice no barriers exist, not for individuals and not for NGOs, not in private litigation and not in judicial review or administrative procedures. Germany (two

1 These interview reports have been included in a separate file, but due to their confidential nature they cannot be published here.

respondents) holds a position at the other side of the scale, especially since even after the *Janecek* and *Trianel* cases individuals still have to prove the impairment of a subjective right to be admitted to environmental proceedings and NGOs still have to be recognised. On the other hand, *procedural barriers* in the UK are much higher than in Germany and Latvia. In the UK, legal representation is mandatory and procedural rules entail high costs. Due to cost-shifting rules (winner takes all) and the indemnity principle, the costs of losing a case (possibly including the premiums of an after-the-event-insurance against a costs order) can be extremely high. Unlike the UK, Germany adopted a system that mitigates costs, that is based on a civil law system and that allows for procedures without legal representation. The same holds for Latvia, where the costs of environmental proceedings are even particularly low.

Thus the three countries provided a background that allowed us to gather diversified information on the possible effects of measures that could be taken. Moreover, at various places in the text we include references to other jurisdictions, notably the Netherlands.

6.4 Assessment of the Interviews

In the following, the diverse elements that have been submitted for comment to the respondents will be briefly characterised and analysed, followed by conclusions based on the views of the respondents and the insights of Chapter 4.

6.4.1 *Definition of Environmental Matters*

Article 9(3) of the Aarhus Convention refers to "national law relating to the environment".[2] The Convention does not define this term, since the definition of "environmental information" in Article 2(3) is clearly not meant to be applied to "law relating to the environment". Article 2(1) subsection (g) of COM(2003) 624 (option 4) final relates the term "environmental law" to implemented Community legislation as specified in that section, leaving it to the Member States to bring national environmental law under the scope of the directive (Art 2(2)).

In Section 4.2.2.1 we stressed the importance of legal certainty. One of the primary objectives of legislation is creating legal certainty, since this will keep costs down, helps avoiding unnecessary costs, leads to an optimal level of judicial intervention and enables the public to make informed choices. From a more general point of view, creating legal certainty is the shared

2 The possibility that "national law" could be interpreted as excluding EU law has been submitted to the respondents, but none of them expected that their national courts would come up with such an interpretation. This matter has therefore been disregarded as not relevant.

advantage of options 3 and 4 over option 1 and 2 (see Section 4.4.3 above). This would imply that a definition of 'environmental' in relation to access to justice has to be considered.

When questioned about this, almost all respondents agreed that providing a definition of environmental matters could be useful. None objected to the idea that this definition would include national law instead of EU law, which is understandable, since Article 9 (3) of the Aarhus Convention is already applicable to national law. Moreover, the link between national and EU law has already been made in the *Slovak brown bear* case. A UK respondent remarked that a definition in a directive would help the national authorities to determine whether a national regulation falls within the scope of Aarhus.

On the other hand, although a definition could be useful, none of the respondents expected that it is actually possible to give a complete and still useful definition. Latvia is doing without such a definition and the courts decide on a case to case basis whether (an aspect of) the case is environmental. This could also lead to the outcome that a case is considered not to be environmental when environmental law is invoked for other purposes than maintaining the environment. The respondent from Scotland made a similar remark, indicating that national peculiarities like the Scottish rights of way and access are too diverse to foresee and risk to be excluded by a definition that is too tight. National lawyers and authorities should keep the possibility to argue that those rights are environmental in a certain sense and thus subject to the provisions of the Aarhus Convention. A respondent from England & Wales concluded that the definition should give a basic guideline, but be open-ended. This coincides with the opinion of other UK respondents, who feared that a definition would easily go beyond Aarhus and that it is better to leave this to the Member States. The German respondents did not have the same opinion: one respondent welcomed a definition and the other argued that a definition is not missed in practice.

When going through all these remarks, the background of the respondents should not be disregarded. Lawyers representing government and operators are hesitant when the possibility of a definition is brought up, whereas lawyers representing NGOs and the public tend to expect benefits from a definition that could prevent long discussions about admissibility and sufficient interest. This leads to the assumption that indeed giving a guiding, but open ended definition, that includes the consequences of the ruling in the *Slovak brown bear* case and bridges the gap between national and EU law in relation to Article 9(3) of the Aarhus Convention (which should be part of option 3), would contribute to the enforcement of environmental law in general.

6.4.2 Private Litigation

Environmental cases need not solely be directed at acts of the administration, but may also be the substance of litigation between private parties. Nuisance cases are a good example, but we might also think of cases in which non-compliance with environmental law gives economic advantages to competitors or cases in which NGOs or individuals bring a lawsuit with the objective to make the defendant comply with environmental regulations. Article 9(3) of the Aarhus Convention stipulates that "members of the public have access to administrative or judicial procedures to challenge acts and omissions by private persons and public authorities which contravene provisions of its national law relating to the environment", but only conditionally, *i.e.* "where they meet the criteria, if any, laid down in (...) national law". When it comes to individuals, there is no provision in the Convention that guarantees access to justice going beyond national law.[3] However, when it comes to organisations and groups, such a provision is certainly included in the Convention for access to justice under Article 9(2), and Article 9(3) is interpreted by the CJEU and also by the Aarhus Convention Compliance Committee in a way as to giving standing rights to NGOs.

Even though the Aarhus Convention does not impose this, some countries (in this study UK and Latvia, but Sweden could also be mentioned as an example) provide for the possibility for individuals to start private litigation merely on the ground that public law (such as environmental regulations) has been breached by the defending party. It turns out that in Latvia this is specifically the case in construction cases, where environmental legislation is invoked to stop building plans. In the UK this led to the "store wars" between supermarkets that try to prevent the entry of a new competitor on the ground that the plans for the new supermarket do not respect environmental legislations. One of the respondents even asserted that 25% of private environmental legislation could be classified as commercial rival type cases.

The situation in countries that require the impairment of a subjective right or sufficient interest for private litigation (like Germany, where the protective norm doctrine applies, and the Netherlands) has not been affected by the Aarhus Convention or the *Slovak brown bear* case. Option 1 would leave matters in this respect unchanged, as would option 4, since COM(2003) 624 did not contain any provisions regarding private litigation. From the interviews it could not be derived that entrusting the public at large with the responsibility for a safe and sound environment yields positive results that could not be obtained otherwise, for instance by leaving it to NGOs or by reporting breaches of environmental law to the competent authorities. To the contrary, environmental law seems to be misused to combat neighbours and commercial rivals. That would call for leaving the current situation unchanged in this respect, even when option 3 is adopted.[4]

---

3 Such a provision can be read in Aarhus for organisations and groups, since it can be derived from the definition of "the public concerned" in Art 2(5). Please note that this term occurs in Art 9(2) but not in Art 9(3). This is the background of the controversy hinted at in the text related to footnote 11 of chapter 2.

4 We should note that the outcome of pending cases such as *Altrip* (C-72/12) might result in a necessity to further clarify (in the directive) the scope of Arts 9(2) and 9(3) as regards access for individuals.

6.4.3 *Suspensive Effect*

Environmental litigation regularly deals with the conformity or non-conformity of decisions of administrative authorities granting permission to start activities that could affect the environment (like planning permissions). Litigation takes time and that means that each jurisdiction will have to provide for mechanisms to prevent that unlawful harm will be done to the environment or that constructors and developers incur losses that are not justified. Therefore, Article 9(4) of the Aarhus Convention stipulates that national law shall provide "adequate and effective (. . .) injunctive relief as appropriate". Several approaches are possible.

In Latvia, commencing proceedings in administrative cases in principle has suspensive effect.[5] The beneficiary of the administrative decision will have to start interim proceedings to obtain permission to start with the project concerned. Since this holds true for all administrative proceedings, the courts appear to be overloaded with applications like these. To get the suspensive effect lifted, two requirements have to be met: a) the administrative decision must be *prima facie* legal and b) the damage caused by the suspensive effect must be considerable without the possibility of compensation afterwards. To deal with all these applications, the courts usually decide them on the written submissions of the parties, without an oral hearing and without investigating the facts of the case. By some this is seen as rather unsatisfactory, since it may lead to incorrect decisions. In practice, it is very hard to get these incorrect decisions reversed. It is believed that making oral hearings obligatory may prevent this. There is no rule that would allow operators to recover damages caused by interim orders from applicants.

The German system could be qualified as multi-layered. Rescissory actions have suspensive effect (Art 80(1) *Verwaltungsgerichtsordnung*), but there are numerous exceptions. In case of such an exception, the administrative authority has the power to order the immediate execution of the decision. This legal situation can be contested by applying for injunctive relief, either by the operator (asking for a 'go ahead' decision), or by the party that thinks the decision is breaching environmental law (thus applying for an interim order against the operator or the administrative authority). German literature is of the opinion that the administration too easily orders immediate execution. Nevertheless, the current situation is considered to be satisfactory, whereas the courts only come in when necessary and will then find a balance between all the conflicting interests, taking into account the probability of the outcome of the case itself and the need for an immediate order. It should be noted that damages caused by interim orders can never be recovered from the applicants, already for the reason that there is no relevant causal relationship between the damage and the application.

5 Exceptions are made, *e.g.* when the application is lodged after expiration of the deadline.

In the UK, like in the Netherlands, starting a judicial review procedure against an administrative decision does not have suspensive effect. The applicant will have to apply for an interim order. Unlike in the Netherlands, in the UK this is not a summary procedure, but involves an extensive oral hearing and is therefore rather costly. The number of applications in environmental matters remains unclear, but the estimations vary from practically none to incidentally (5-10% of the cases). Damages resulting from interim relief can be recovered from the applicant if the court gives an order to that end (cross-undertaking in damages). Some think this is beneficial, because offering to pay damages will help to get interim relief; others see this as the cause that interim relief is never applied for, since the risk of having to pay damages adds to the already high costs of the possibility of future bankruptcy. On the other hand, it is argued that a fear for Pyrrhic victories (winning the case after the highway has been built) is unfounded, since investors will not spend huge amounts of money when permissions can be overturned in the future.
Making a choice to guide the various systems could help protecting the environment. In fact, Article 9(4) of the Aarhus Convention seems to indicate that also injunctive relief should be "fair, equitable, timely and not prohibitively expensive". Since interim orders can be obtained in each of the countries, the only question that remains is whether each of these systems is equally compatible with the said provision. The proposed directive COM(2003) 624 was rather neutral in this respect, since it did no more than repeating the words of the convention (Art 10) and provide that "members of the public" should have access to injunctive relief (Art 4).

From the point of view of law and economics, law can only be effective when the incentives for stakeholders help them to make decisions in accordance with the goals that are set. The judiciary should therefore at least be stimulated to take the proper interests into account (private interests of all parties concerned and the public interest of environmental protection), which will necessitate an oral hearing if the urgency of the case does not preclude this. Starting from our observations in Chapter 4, there is no economic model that will not predict that cross-undertakings in damages will prevent applicants from submitting their application for interim relief to the court. It seems therefore that a ban (possibly with provisos) on these cross-undertakings is indispensable for an effective implementation of the Aarhus Convention. Both observations call for option 3, since these rules will have to be part of a new directive and cannot be realised in any other way.

6.4.4 *Outcome of Proceedings*

Environmental litigation in a public law setting will always be directed against decisions of administrative authorities. This touches on a sensitive nerve of modern democratic states, since this type of litigation directly involves the relationship between the judiciary and the administration. This implies that the courts will have to keep distances from what is considered to be the exclusive realm of the administration. This consequence of the separation of powers (or a system of checks and balances) restricts the possible forms of relief.

In the Netherlands, the matter is solved by instructing the courts to investigate the legality of the decision, supplemented with an extensive reasonableness test. This leaves room for judicial interference in cases in which procedural or substantive shortcomings occur. The courts have the power to quash the decision and to send the matter back to the administration, but may also – in cases in which the legally correct outcome is not disputable – substitute the decision of the administration with its own. This can be combined with rewarding a claim for damages against the administration.

The courts in the countries involved in this survey seem to be slightly more restricted. They have full powers to rule on the legality of a decision and to assess the procedure that has been followed (whether the facts have been assessed correctly, whether all interests have been taken into account), but substituting the decision of the administration is not possible. German courts may give side orders (*Nebenbestimmungen*) regarding the way the case has to be handled in the future, which could also be directed towards third parties such as operators. This is considered to be a useful tool. In Latvia, the administrative procedure can be combined with a claim for damages against the administrative authority.

Although there are some differences, all respondents answered that in their opinion sufficient relief could be obtained in the procedures that are available to challenge environmental decisions. Apparently, these remedies are considered to be 'adequate and effective' in the sense of Article 9(4) of the Aarhus Convention. Within the national jurisdictions there is very little room for change, since this matter touches on the essence of a democratic society under the rule of law. Even when choosing option 3, this means that the current situation should be respected.

However, one issue has not really been investigated and deserves some consideration. One of the Latvian respondents reflected on the possibility of bringing things back in the old situation when, after some years of litigation, it turns out that the permission that was used by the operator was not legally sound after all. This was considered as only hypothetically possible, since probably the courts will not be willing to accept an immense waste of costs to further some environmental interest. Speaking in terms of Calabresi and Melamed (1972) this would mean that these interests are only protected with a liability rule (the common good can be wasted against payment of damages) or no rule at all (since maybe there is no claimant who suffered the damages). Strictly spoken, this cannot be labelled as 'adequate and effective'. Measures to prevent the coming into being of such a situation call for taking recourse to option 3.

6.4.5 *System Costs*

It turned out to be impossible to assess the system costs (costs for the judiciary and administration) for any of the options as such or even for the constituent elements thereof that were discussed with the respondents. None of the selected countries maintains court statistics in which environmental cases are categorised separately. Statements about the possible increase or decrease of these cases can therefore not be made without substantial additional research. This could be an argument for choosing option 3 rather than option 4, since the original proposal asks for national reports (Art 11), but does not specify the contents of these reports. These should at least contain information about the number of Aarhus cases.

However, the interviews gave some remarkable insights in the working of the access to justice provisions in the selected countries. The statement of one of the respondents that "the danger of widening standing has always been exaggerated" is confirmed rather than falsified. When taking the cases of England & Wales and Latvia, one would rather reach the opposite conclusion. Latvia has wide access to justice and practically no barriers at all, whereas England & Wales share the aspect of wide access, but litigating there is anyhow very expensive. Nevertheless, the number of environmental cases is much higher in England & Wales than in Latvia, even in proportion to the population. This seems to indicate that standing requirements as such will not have serious consequences for system costs and neither do party-friendly litigating arrangements (no mandatory representation, low court fees, inquisitorial courts).

The Latvian case asks for some explanation. Like the Scottish respondent for her jurisdiction, all Latvian respondents supposed that it is partly a matter of mentality. Latvian people are not accustomed to use the law as an instrument to combat the government and fellow citizens in order to reach their goals. But it was also pointed out that good eNGOs channel discontentment in a very efficient way: eNGOs that have enough expertise at their disposal and are based in society will be relied on by other parties whose environmental interests are affected. This results in a funnel and sieve effect, with the consequence that a single eNGO can voice the arguments of all people involved in one single procedure. Remarks along the same vein have been made by the German respondents.

When making a choice between the four options central in this report, the finding above provides a clear guideline. Facilitating access to justice is unlikely to lead to an overburdened judicial system, when at the same time the position of eNGOs as serious partners in the enforcement of environmental law is secured. Consequently, option 3 seems to be the best way to take, since it allows the combination of widening access in accordance with the Aarhus Convention and strengthening the position of eNGOs that are to be considered as serious partners.

6.4.6 *Requirements NGOs*

The system that the Aarhus Convention imposes is that NGOs meeting certain requirements must have free access to justice in environmental matters, since these NGOs are deemed to have a sufficient interest (Art 9(3) jo. Art 2(5) last sentence). National law may impose criteria (Art 9(3)), but obviously these criteria should satisfy the requirements of Article 9(4) and should not in fact impair the essence of the rights that are awarded to these NGOs. The ECJ case law mentioned above (especially *Djurgården*) showed for instance that a requirement setting the minimum number of members at 2000 is not compatible with the objectives set forth by the Aarhus Convention as implemented by Directive 2003/35 EC.

The proposed directive COM(2003) 624 gave extensive rules for the recognition of NGOs (called "entities"). Article 8 provided for the criteria. To qualify for recognition, a NGO should a) be an independent and non-profit-making legal person,which has the objective to protect the environment; b) have an organisational structure which enables it to ensure the adequate pursuit of its statutory objectives; c) have been legally constituted and have been working actively for environmental protection, in conformity with its statutes, for a period to be fixed by the Member State in which is constituted, but not exceeding three years; d) have its annual statement of accounts certified by a registered auditor for a period to be fixed by each Member State. Article 9 gave the choice between two procedures for recognition, a preliminary procedure and an ad hoc case by case recognition. Each State had to ensure that there is always a possibility for an expeditious "ad hoc" recognition.

The basis for these provisions in the Aarhus Convention is rather narrow, if not non-existent. The convention leaves it to the Member States to set the requirements and leaves open the possibility that no requirements will apply. From this point of view, the proposal could be seen as a step back. The differences in Europe are reflected in the actual situation in the selected countries, where Latvia and England & Wales (and Scotland as well) have very wide standing rules that allow all NGOs to start environmental proceedings, including *ad hoc* NGOs and transborder litigation, without being required to go through a recognition procedure of any kind. Germany on the other hand requires recognition in advance. The recognition is granted by the federal Environment Ministry on basis of the *Umwelt-Rechtsbehelfsgesetz*. The main conditions for the recognition are that the association must, according to its articles of association, support nature protection and landscape conservation aims in a durable manner, have actively existed for at least three years at the time of the application, pursue its tasks in a proper manner and be based on open membership.

The arguments put forward for this recognition by the German respondents concentrate mainly on the importance of guaranteeing that NGOs are serious partners in environmental protection. *Ad hoc* NGOs are excluded but this can be circumvented by finding a neighbouring landowner who is willing to lend his name and interests to start proceedings. Working on a case by case basis is seen as a poor alternative. It can be added that a recognition procedure may prevent the problems that arose in Latvia where an ad hoc NGO used environmental proceedings to blackmail an operator without pursuing any genuine environmental interests.

This is not the place to discuss the right requirements, which is a subject that is a point of focus of the Aarhus Compliance Committee and is addressed in the Implementation Guide.[6] Also, the recent Darpö study on effective access to justice provides some recommendations on this.[7] We can limit ourselves to the observation that liberal access to justice rules for NGOs will not have serious effects on system costs, when these NGOs are good partners in the enforcement of environmental law. Therefore, a thorough consideration of these requirements is called for. Probably a good solution would be to draft provisions to safeguard the quality and continuity of environmental NGOs without imposing strict conditions. That leaves the choice of the best options to the Member States, which are thus enabled to take their domestic circumstances into account and also gives them the opportunity to give full discretion to the courts in combination with extremely liberal standing rules. Obviously, option 3 gives the best opportunity to realise this.

6.4.7 *Actio Popularis*

The preceding paragraphs indicated that wide standing rules will not lead to significant system costs, provided that representative and professional NGOs channel concerns regarding the enforcement of environmental law. This can be supplemented by the observation that an increase in the number of procedures is not necessarily a bad thing. Where negative externalities are not likely but might occur to an insignificant degree, they will be outweighed by positive externalities like acquiring more 'public goods' in the form of court opinions and the enhanced enforcement of environmental law.

It has already been observed that dropping standing requirements for individuals is not something of which only good results can be expected. A carefully designed new directive should find a midway solution by defining selection mechanisms to filter out the right NGOs and make those NGOs profit from the liberal standing rules of the Aarhus Convention. This solution can only be embedded when option 3 is chosen.

---

6 See <www.unece.org/fileadmin/DAM/env/pp/mop4/Documents/Implementation.Guide.21.06.2011.track-changes.pdf>.

7 See the Synthesis report 'Effective Justice' of the Darpö study, available at: <http://ec.europa.eu/environment/aarhus/pdf/2012_access_justice_report.pdf>.

6.4.8 *Costs*

Article 9(4) of the Aarhus Convention provides that environmental procedures "shall provide adequate and effective remedies (...) and be fair, equitable, timely and not prohibitively expensive". The last part of this provision raises the question when proceedings are so expensive that they form a barrier to start proceedings and prevent the members of the public from seeking review in environmental cases. This is a complex question, which can only be answered when all relevant costs and benefits are taken into consideration. The aspects that come to mind are court fees, salaries of legal representatives (solicitors, barristers, advocates), the necessity of legal representation, the costs of expertise and witnesses, and costs orders.

There are enormous differences between distinct Member States. On the one hand there are Latvia and the Netherlands with low court fees (frequently not exceeding € 100), no need for legal representation, State-paid expertise and no costs orders against plaintiffs in administrative proceedings. Probably a procedure about the legality of a complicated planning permission will cost an NGO that has enough expertise to be represented in court by one of its own employees in these countries not more than € 1,000, even when they lose. On the other hand, in the United Kingdom challenging of administrative decisions takes the form of judicial review, which is a highly complicated procedure with mandatory legal representation, expert costs to be paid by the parties and costs orders against the losing party that encompass all costs actually made by the other party. A conservative estimation of the total costs in case of loss will easily exceed an amount of £ 100,000. Germany is somewhere in between but on the low side, since costs are related to the disputed value (*Streitwert*) and this disputed value is set rather low, even when the procedure is about a € 2 billion coal power plant. However, expert costs are paid by the parties and not by the State.

This 1:100 ratio already gives an indication that probably environmental litigation in the UK is prohibitively expensive in the meaning of Article 9(4) of the Aarhus Convention. Measures like PCOs (protective costs orders) can hardly be effective, since the caps are set rather high (£ 20,000-30,000) and are often accompanied by a cross-cap. This means that a winning plaintiff will only get £ 10,000 (or the actual amount of the cross-cap) of all the costs and expenses that have been made. Since cases like these are usually litigated on the basis of conditional fee agreements, it will according to some interviewees be very difficult to find a solicitor to handle the case, since the uplift can certainly not be collected and thus the solicitor will never get the compensation for the cases that he will not win.

Article 10 of the proposal COM(2003) 624 did no more than repeating the words of the Aarhus Convention. This can hardly be enough. Case C-260/11 (*Edwards*) is now pending before the Court of Justice of the European Union, in which the UK Supreme Court submitted the question which costs are still acceptable in environmental proceedings. The conclusion of Advocate-General Kokott was published on 18 October 2012. He first advised the Court to rule that

> it is in principle for the Member States to determine how to avoid the judicial proceedings covered not being conducted on account of their costs. However, those measures must ensure in a sufficiently clear and binding manner that the objectives of the Aarhus Convention are satisfied in each individual case and, at the same time, observe the principles of effectiveness and equivalence and the fundamental rights under EU law.

This corresponds with his observation that the interpretation of the concept of "prohibitively expensive" cannot be left to the Member States (para. 25). As to the actual costs that are acceptable, the Advocate-General sets out some points of reference that have to be taken into account when assessing the costs:

> The answer to the second question [should the costs question be examined on a subjective or an objective basis]is therefore that in examining whether costs of proceedings are prohibitive, account must be taken of the objective and subjective circumstances of the case, with the aim of enabling wide access to justice. The insufficient financial capacity of the claimant may not constitute an obstacle to proceedings. It is necessary always, hence including when determining the costs which can be expected of claimants having capacity to pay, to take due account of the public interest in environmental protection in the case at issue.

Whatever the court ruling may be, it is clear that guidelines in a possible new directive could clarify the current situation and provide the principles underlying the measures that are "sufficiently clear and binding" to keep costs within the boundaries set by the Aarhus Convention. Especially the public interest that has to be taken into account needs a form of quantification that will easily be lost out of sight when personal circumstances are overemphasised. Costs can be prohibitively expensive even when a plaintiff has enough means to pay them, *i.e.* when the personal benefits of the plaintiff when winning the case do not outweigh the total of the transaction costs that are to be made. The public interest as defined and quantified by a new directive could compensate for this. Here again, option 3 would be the best option, especially since there are many ways to reduce system costs in the countries concerned, for instance by moving environmental litigation outside the jurisdiction of the common law courts.

6.4.9 *Third Party Protection and Frivolous Claims*

When designing this survey, it was supposed that third parties should not be overlooked in environmental proceedings. When an administrative decision is challenged, the beneficiary of that decision should be heard, and in the case of private litigation between a member of the public and an operator, the administration should have the opportunity to intervene when the public interest is at stake.

The outcome of the interviews was clear. In each of the selected countries the interests of third parties were adequately protected. This leads to option 1, or to option 3 or 4, since no measures in this respect have been foreseen.

The same goes for measures to obviate frivolous claims. The respondents were not aware of any serious problems in this respect, even though no specific measures, not already part of procedural law as a whole, had been taken.

6.4.10 *Levelling the Playing Field*

In Chapter 4 we put forward the hypothesis that operators might welcome the idea that the level of environmental protection and enforcement of environmental law would be the same in all EU Member States. Although this would unmistakably have some advantages over cross-border disparities, it does not follow automatically that industry itself would welcome a directive that ensures a wider access to justice in environmental matters. In fact, interviewees turned out to be unanimous in their opinion that operators would, after all, prefer the current situation and thus option 1, as imperfect as it may be.

6.4.11 *Mediation*

In environmental matters, the advantage of mediation would not be staying out of court, but finding solutions that do justice to all interests at stake, especially the interests of the environment itself. In an exchange of ideas between the public, operators and the administration in a setting where proceedings are possible, but not inevitable, solutions may be found that could not be discussed in the public consultation phase. From the point of view of law and economics, such a solution would almost only have advantages (see Section 4.3.4.2 above).

In general, the respondents were quite positive towards mediation. However, it became clear that not all environmental conflicts are suitable for mediation. When an interpretative ruling is needed, only court proceedings offer a solution to the conflict. Moreover, some hesitations were expressed concerning the margins available to the administration in a mediation setting. In some cases, the administration has no room of appreciation and civil servants could have a tendency to rely on the backing of a court decision rather than taking responsibility of their own.

Promoting mediation could be a valuable and useful objective of a new directive. The effectiveness will depend on the method used to select conflicts that mediation could solve. Otherwise, inciting stakeholders to mediate that is bound to fail would only enhance costs and reduce the effectiveness of environmental law.

7 Summary and Policy Recommendations

Michael Faure and Niels Philipsen

In this final chapter, we summarise the main findings and provide some (carefully formulated) policy suggestions. The set-up is as follows: first, we repeat the goals of this study and the main set-up (1), followed by a summary of our main findings (2). We then move briefly beyond the scope of the original research questions by showing on the one hand some limits of the research, and on the other hand a few points identified by the interviewees, which were not originally addressed by us but which may be worth examining (3). We conclude the chapter by offering a few policy recommendations (4).

7.1 Goals of the Research

The main goals of this book were the following:

- To highlight the differences between the four options mentioned in the introduction from an economic perspective, taking into account that some EU Member States may anyway be forced to adapt their national system on the basis of recent CJEU case law. The marginal costs of awarding more access to justice (via a harmonised regime in a directive) may be minimal, whereas marginal benefits (in the sense of reducing uncertainty, internalising externalities, and creating a level playing field) may be huge.
- To investigate to what extent the absence of an EU-wide regime for access to justice in environmental matters is in fact disadvantageous for operators. Economic and other arguments could be provided that (more particularly taking into account recent evolutions in case law) non-action can create substantial uncertainty and differences between Member States which are costly for operators. An EU-wide system would then have the advantage of creating legal certainty and hence levelling the playing field.

We want to repeat that the goal of our study was not to examine, *e.g.* to what extent Member States accurately implemented the environmental *acquis* with respect to access to justice, nor the Aarhus Convention. The added value of our research is rather that the various options of access to justice (*i.e.* the four options mentioned in the introduction and elaborated on in Chapter 3) were examined from a socio-economic perspective.

The idea was to reach the goal of this research through a combination of various approaches:

- Theoretical analysis, divided into a legal, Law and Economics, and short Law and Society part, and resulting in hypotheses that are tested in the empirical analysis.

- Empirical analysis, testing the results obtained in the theoretical study by means of interviews and (where possible) collection of available empirical data. The empirical analysis is crucial since it provides indications on how stakeholders experience the differences between the four options. The results of these empirical studies in the Member States will hence to an important extent feed the policy recommendations.

7.2 Main Findings

The report started by examining the status quo of access to justice in environmental matters and more particularly the case law of the CJEU. In Chapter 2 we sketched that case law based on Directive 2003/35/EC provides a broad interpretation of the possibilities of access to justice in the areas where the EIA and IPPC Directives apply. However, it was also shown that the interpretation and application of Article 9(2) of the Aarhus Convention still significantly differs in the Member States.

The most important development in case law comes from the *Slovak brown bear* case. This recent case forces national courts to interpret law as much as possible in such a way as to enable environmental NGOs, in line with Article 9(3) of the Aarhus Convention, to challenge administrative environmental decisions in Member States. However, this case alone will not lead to a full application of Article 9(3) since substantial differences between EU Member States in the application of Article 9(3) do exist and are likely to remain. However, an important conclusion from Chapter 2 is that many Member States may anyway be forced to bring their national legislation in line with the obligations resulting from the Aarhus Convention as interpreted by the ECJ.

After examining more closely the four options for regulating access to justice in environmental matters in Chapter 3, we presented the economic analysis of access to justice and the application to the Aarhus Convention in Chapter 4. Several perspectives were presented, including not only a welfare economic analysis, but also a behavioural approach. In that respect, the question how different rules affect the incentives of stakeholders received particular attention. Starting point of the economic analysis is that access to justice is considered positively, provided that such access does not lead to frivolous litigation. Environmental harm is seen as a negative externality which can be reduced by litigation. A judgment can be considered as a public good (since others than the parties involved may benefit from it) and when, *e.g.* injunctive relief is awarded (prohibiting, *e.g.* the legal installation of a harmful activity) such a decision can generate positive externalities. However, economists also stress that cases may generate high costs and therefore they strongly advocate settlements over trials. We also paid attention to the behavioural Law and Economics literature which addresses how particular biases and heuristics may affect the behaviour of the judiciary, and how this may lead potential plaintiffs not to bring particular suits as a result of which social welfare would not be maximised. Standing for NGOs is from an economic perspective considered as positive since it can remedy the 'rational apathy' problem that may emerge when the damage has a very widespread character, an argument that often applies to environmental harm. The same rationale that justifies class actions in case of consumer losses of a scattered nature also justifies standing for environmental NGOs, again under the important condition that these eNGOs serve a public interest goal.

Next, we analysed how the four options will affect the incentives of the various stakeholders involved. In that respect, we concluded that the first two options (business as usual and addressing existing gaps via case law) have the disadvantage that legal uncertainty will to a large extent remain. Options 3 and 4 both rely on the creation of a new directive, which is likely to reduce uncertainty costs. In both options access to justice would be enlarged, especially in option 4 (sticking to the original proposal COM(2003) 624). This may potentially even lead to overdeterrence where questions could arise as a result of the broad scope of the proposal. This could hence lead to a slight preference for option 3 (drafting a new legislative proposal taking into account the recent case law).

Finally, the economic analysis added an additional perspective by looking at the extent to which the various options create a level playing field for industry and plaintiffs. Theoretically, differences between Member States as far as access to justice in environmental matters is concerned, could endanger the level playing field. As Table 4.1 in Section 4.4.5 made clear, options 1 and 2 do not guarantee a level playing field, whereas this is more likely under options 3 and 4. However, in option 4 cross-border NGO standing would not be regulated. This would hence once more suggest a slight preference for option 3.

The advantage of option 3 is that compared to options 1 and 2 it provides more legal certainty and that there may be a higher deterrent effect in terms of internalising environmental externalities. In economic terms option 3 may even lead to an optimal number of suits, while it would be less costly than option 2, since calls on the CJEU could be avoided. Option 3 might also have the advantage compared to option 4 that it is less controversial, given the high opposition that originally occurred against proposal COM(2003) 624. Option 3 potentially also has the advantage of creating fewer possibilities for strategic behaviour by NGOs, and less of a danger of overdeterrence. It excludes *e.g.* a reference to "all administrative acts and omissions" and explicit criteria for recognition of NGOs. Also the environmental mediation that could be included in option 3 could (under specific conditions) have the advantage of creating a low-cost alternative compared to the court system.

Having provided an economic analysis in Chapter 4, we turned to a brief alternative approach to access to justice, based on Law and Society. This approach enlightened why generally a requirement of *locus standi* may be necessary. It also showed that sticking to a very strict standing requirement and hence restricting access to justice may not be in the public interest in the environmental cases we addressed in this study. When the Law and Society literature is related to the four options, again options 1 and 2 do not seem very appealing. These options would not bring legal certainty, but may rather result in an extremely diverse legal environment. Option 4 could have advantages, but given the opposition to the Commission's original proposal, this option may not be realistic, even when taking into account that there is now some CJEU case law. Hence, at the end of Chapter 5, we argued that option 3 may represent the "best of both worlds" by allowing an implementation of case law and the environmental *acquis* with respect to access to justice, while at the same time preserving some regulatory autonomy for the Member States. However, in order to make environmental access to justice work, it is important to develop a genuine legal culture in favour of environmental Public Interest Litigation. Hence, lawyers and civil society organisations could accompany the process of implementing option 3.

Chapter 6 presented the empirical part of the research and more particularly the country studies relating to Latvia, the United Kingdom and Germany.[1] The goal of the country studies was to test the hypotheses formulated in the earlier chapters and more particularly to examine the preferences of stakeholders (plaintiffs, operators, administrative authorities, judiciary) in the Member States with regard to the four regulatory options central to this study. Rather than asking interviewees to react to these options directly, specific elements that are part of one or more of these options were discussed, such as suspensive effect, possible outcomes of proceedings, system costs, requirements for eNGOs and litigation between private parties.

Interestingly, all interviewees held that it could be useful to provide a definition of the concept 'environmental matters', to which Article 9(3) of the Aarhus Convention refers. This follows up on the importance of legal certainty that was explicitly mentioned in the economic analysis (in Section 4.2.2.1). On the other hand, no one objected that this definition would follow from national law rather than EU law. Currently *e.g.* Latvia is doing without such a definition and decides on a case-to-case basis whether (an aspect of) the case is environmental, apparently not leading to large difficulties.

Latvia and the UK have broad standing rules. Latvia moreover has very low costs for access to justice. Despite the combination of broad standing rules and low costs, there have been few environmental cases in Latvia. Various possible explanations for that result were provided; an important one seems to be the quality and functioning of environmental NGOs. Well-functioning eNGOs are (according to Latvian respondents) able to bundle and channel environmental complaints, rather than creating excessive litigation.

Only Germany has particular demands as far as the recognition of NGOs is concerned. As such, the Aarhus Convention allows this. If option 3 were followed, one could consider

1 Portugal was on the list also, but respondents could not be found.

that the new directive provides particular minimum requirements for eNGOs. These requirements could guarantee that eNGOs indeed act for the goal for which they have been created.

The economic notion of legal certainty is, as we mentioned earlier, an important issue for many respondents in the countries we analysed. Surprisingly, however, the respondents did not expect that "leveling the playing field" would be considered as a major issue for enterprises. It was generally believed that the less enterprises are hindered by eNGOs, the better. However, it was not held that differences in that respect between Member States constitute a major argument in favor of harmonisation. Reducing legal certainty, however, would.

Summarising, although some other issues (see below) came out of the interviews than we expected, to a large extent the interviews confirmed the preference for option 3 which also came out of the theoretical analysis in Chapters 4 and 5. A new directive (option 3) would have the advantage of *e.g.* providing some requirements for the functioning of NGOs. This would at the same time allow NGOs to have the positive function of streamlining and channeling social unrest and thereby preventing litigation. From that perspective, *locus standi* for environmental NGOs (not necessarily for individuals) would not be problematic and could be realised via option 3.

7.3 Beyond the Current Research

As we indicated in Chapter 6, to some extent the interviews led to additional insights that were not mentioned explicitly in the theoretical analysis of Chapters 4 and 5. On the one hand, we noticed some limits in the ability of interviewees to analyse the various options (especially option 3: a new or substantially modified directive); on the other hand, highly interesting information came out which in fact points at important issues that need to be taken into account in order to guarantee an effective access to justice in environmental matters. That may, hence, once more underscore the attractiveness of option 3 since a new directive may precisely allow the regulation of some of those issues.

A first point to be repeated is that our study was limited to an economic analysis of various options of (increasing) environmental access to justice. Specific legal issues were not addressed, since they were part of a recent study by Darpö and others. They may, however, be quite important in the policy context. For example, we showed in Chapter 2 that there is discussion on the precise interpretation of some of the ECJ case law. On these issues we obviously did not take a particular stand.

Also, it may have been interesting to compare the pre-2003/35/EC situation with the situation in Member States after the transposition of Directive 2003/35/EC, because the introduction of a new directive (option 3 or 4) may have similar effects. However, access to justice in environmental matters is not only dependent upon the application of this directive, given its limited scope, and respondents in Member States had limited information in that respect.

A related and important issue is that many respondents held that the real question of effective access to justice in environmental matters does not only depend on the formal legal rules (*e.g.* on standing) but also on other factors which one could summarise as legal culture. This corresponds with the Law and Society analysis from Chapter 5, where it was equally stressed that the legal culture in a particular country may be of particular importance in stimulating access to justice in environmental matters. Related issues that came out of the interviews in the country studies were *e.g.* the importance of the costs of access to justice. This is, from a Law and Economics perspective, an important point. It also fits in with Article 9(4) of the Aarhus Convention, which makes the cost issue also a legal point. The country study for the United Kingdom showed that costs of litigation generally and also in environmental matters are often prohibitively high. The question in that respect could be asked whether, within a framework of transposing Article 9(4) of the Aarhus Convention in option 3 (drafting a new directive), also attention to the cost issue should be paid. A related issue is that when an environmental NGO claims a suspension of a particular activity via injunctive relief, this could (*e.g.* in the UK) lead to liability of the plaintiff for the costs resulting from the delay. One does not have to be a great Law and Economics scholar to realise that this may seriously limit the incentives of plaintiffs to file meritorious suits. Again, within the framework of option 3, the question arises if one should regulate the fact that access to justice cannot lead to potential liability of plaintiffs, since this may unduly jeopardise access to justice.

Another striking issue in the United Kingdom relates to the fact that 25% of all environmental cases in the UK are not launched by individual victims or environmental NGOs, but by other companies (so-called "store wars"). This is obviously a downside of enlarged access to justice, but it is not likely that any type of regulation could prevent this.

7.4 Recommendations

Some of the recommendations at the policy level follow logically from the issues mentioned in this chapter so far:

7.4.1 Opt for Option 3

This conclusion follows logically from the theoretical analysis in Chapters 4 and 5. Option 3 (drafting a new directive incorporating the recent case law enlarging access to justice) will have the advantage of creating legal certainty and (even though this was not considered a main issue by respondents in the country studies) will allow a levelling of the playing field. Options 1 and 2 do not create legal certainty and option 4 may lead to overdeterrence and may politically be less feasible. Hence, also from the Law and Society perspective in Chapter 5, option 3 was preferred.

Option 3 also came out as the most appealing one from the comparative research, in fact for the simple reason that there may be a number of issues that could affect the effectiveness of access to justice in environmental matters and that hence could be regulated in a new directive, which is only possible under option 3.

Some of the issues that could (but not necessarily must) be regulated in such a directive relate to the other recommendations. We formulate those with a slight degree of caution. The reason is that most of those recommendations are based on reactions from respondents during the interviews and hence they have not been subject of thorough theoretical research. In this respect, we mainly mention that those points are according to respondents of importance. Whether they can be dealt with at national law or should be dealt with at EU level, let alone be incorporated in a new directive, is still another matter that could perhaps be subject of further research. We now merely mention those points as recommendations in the sense that they need attention, at what level and how this should lead to regulation is an issue that was not explicitly analysed in this research. That is why the remaining recommendations should be read with caution.

7.4.2 Define Environmental Matters

Most interviewees held that it may be useful to provide a more precise definition of what the environmental matters are to which Article 9(3) of the Aarhus Convention would be applicable. It can be seen by the *Slovak brown bear* case that application of Article 9(3) was accepted under the Habitats Directive but there are some question marks as to what are the actual limits and if this is to be interpreted the same way under the full breadth of EU environmental law. A Directive could indeed provide certainty in this regard by a definition. However, as we indicated, respondents also mention that this could eventually be defined in national law. Very complex and detailed definitions are probably not necessary; Latvia is currently doing without such a definition and decides the applicability on a case-by-case basis, which is apparently not leading to large difficulties.

However, a question one could ask is to what extent one wishes to exclude access to environmental matters for companies suing each other in private litigation. We believe that this may be some unavoidable consequence of enlarging access to justice, but that it should not necessarily lead to an exclusion of this type of litigation. Drafting this may be extremely difficult. Moreover, the negative effects for society of this private litigation are not immediately clear. Even if it is a competitor who sues as a plaintiff, as long as the suit is brought for an enforcement of environmental law, negative externalities (through the violation of environmental legislation) may be remedied and positive externalities (via judgments clarifying the application of the law) may be generated. Hence, we would be cautious with a legislative intervention excluding access to justice in case of private litigation.

7.4.3 Stimulate the Functioning of Environmental NGOs

The cases of Latvia and the UK showed that a large standing for environmental NGOs does not lead to more cases. Quite to the contrary, well-functioning environmental NGOs show to be able to channel social unrest and hence precisely prevent an explosion of cases.

7.4.4 Reduce Costs and Risks for Plaintiffs

If one wishes at the policy level to stimulate access to justice in environmental matters, it may not be sufficient merely to change substantive or procedural rules. In the spirit of Article 9(4) of the Aarhus Convention, one also has to make sure that procedures are not prohibitively expensive. At this moment, we suffice by mentioning that in some of the Member States (the UK for example) this may be a problem and that hence the cost issue surely deserves attention.

By the same token, the reduction of risks for plaintiffs deserves attention as well. If, when asking injunctive relief, plaintiffs could be exposed to potential liability for the results of their action, this would seriously jeopardise access to justice. Again, we do not at this stage go as far as to immediately plead for an immunity of liability for plaintiffs in environmental cases. We merely point out that attention should be paid to the potentially negative effects of liabilities imposed on plaintiffs in environmental matters.

7.4.5 Stimulate Access to Justice in Environmental Matters Generally

Our final recommendation comes from the Law and Society movement: that literature has stressed that a greater access to justice will not necessarily lead to a better implementation of the existing environmental rules if nothing is done additionally in terms of awareness raising and training of judges, lawyers, NGOs and businesses. Hence, we recommend that any formal change in legislation is at the same time accompanied by measures that will promote a behavioural change as far as the legal culture promoting access to justice in environmental matters and compliance with (European) environmental law is concerned.

Bibliography

Allen, D.W. (2000), "Transaction Costs", in Bouckaert, B. & De Geest, G. (eds), *Encyclopedia of Law and Economics*, Volume V, Cheltenham, UK and Northampton, MA: Edward Elgar, pp. 893-926.

Andhyarujina, T.R. (2011), *The Kesavananda Bharati Case: the Untold Story of Struggle for Supremacy by Supreme Court and Parliament,* Universal Law Publishing.

Bakkes, J.A., Bräuer, I., Ten Brink, P., Görlach, B., Kuik, O.J. & Medhurst, J. (2008), *Cost of Policy Inaction, Scoping Study for DG Environment*, MNP / IEEP / Ecologic / IvM / GHK.

Barrow, D.J. & Zuk, G. (1990), "An Institutional Analysis of Turnover in the Lower Federal Courts", *The Journal of Politics*, 52 (2), pp. 457-476.

Baxi, U. (1985), "Taking Suffering Seriously: Social Action Litigation in the Supreme Court of India", *Third World Legal Studies*, 4 (1), pp. 107-132.

Bebchuk, L.A. (1984), "Litigation and Settlement under Imperfect Information", *RAND Journal of Economics*, 15, pp. 404-415.

Bebchuk, L.A. (1988), "Suing, Solely to Extract a Settlement Offer", *Journal of Legal Studies*, 17, pp. 437-450.

Bebchuk, L.A. (1996), "A New Theory Concerning the Credibility and Success of Threats to Sue", *Journal of Legal Studies*, 25, pp. 1-25.

Becker, G.S. (1968), "Crime and Punishment: An Economic Approach", *Journal of Political Economy*, 76, pp. 169-217.

Becker, R. & Henderson, J.V. (2000), "Effects of Air Quality Regulations on Polluting Industries", *Journal of Political Economy*, 108 (2), pp. 379-421.

Beenstock, M. & Haitovsky, Y. (2004), "Does the Appointment of Judges Increase the Output of the Judiciary?", *International Review of Law and Economics*, 24, pp. 351-369.

Bernstein, L. (1992), "Opting out of the Legal System: Extralegal Contractual Relations in the Diamond Industry", *Journal of Legal Studies*, 21, pp. 115-157.

Bernstein, R. (1978), "Judicial Economy and Class Action", *Journal of Legal Studies*, 7, pp. 349-370.

Block, M.K., Parker, J.S., Vyborna, O. & Ducek, L. (2000), "An Experimental Comparison of Adversial versus Inquisitorial Procedural Regimes", *American Law and Economics Review*, 2, pp. 170-194.

Blume, L.E. & Rubinfeld, D.L. (1982), "The Dynamics of the Legal Process", *Journal of Legal Studies*, 11, pp. 405-419.

Bowles, R. (1987), "Settlement Range and Cost Allocation Rules: A Comment on Avery Katz's Measuring the Demand for Litigation: Is the English Rule Really Cheaper?", *Journal of Law and Economics*, 3, pp. 177-184.

Calabresi, G. & Melamed, A.D. (1972), "Property Rules, Liability Rules and Inalienability: One View of the Cathedral", *Harvard Law Review*, 85 (6), pp. 1089-1128.

Cooter, R.D. (1983), "The Objectives of Private and Public Judges", *Public Choice*, 41, pp. 107-132.

Cooter, R.D. & Rubinfeld, D.L. (1989), "Economic Analysis of Legal Disputes and Their Resolution", *Journal of Economic Literature*, 27, pp. 1067-1097.

Cooter, R.D. & Rubinfeld, D.L. (1990), "Trial Courts: An Economic Perspective", *Law & Society Review*, 24, pp. 533-548.

Cooter, R.D. & Ulen, T. (2011), *Law and Economics*, 6th international edn, Boston, MA: Pearson

Danzon, P.M. & Lillard, L.A. (1983), "Settlement out of Court: The Disposition of Medical Malpractice Claims", *Journal of Legal Studies*, 12, pp. 345-377.

DasGupta, M. (2009), *Courting Development: The Supreme Court, Public Interest Litigation and Socio-Economic Development in India*, VDM Verlag.

Dasgupta, S., Laplante, B., Wang, H. & Wheeler, D. (2002), "Confronting the Environmental Kuznets Curve", *Journal of Economic Perspectives*, 16 (1), pp. 147-168.

De Sadeleer, N., Roller, G. & Dross, M. (2005) (eds), *Access to Justice in Environmental Matters and the Role of NGOs. Empirical Findings and Legal Appraisal*, Groningen: Europa Law Publishing.

Divan, S. & Rosencranz, A. (2001), *Environmental Law and Policy in India: Cases, Materials and Statutes*, 2nd edn, New Delhi: Oxford University Press.

Ebbeson, J. (2011), "Access to Justice at a National Level. Impact of the Aarhus Convention and European Union Law", in Pallemaerts, M. (ed.), *The Aarhus Convention at Ten. Interactions and Tensions between Conventional International Law and EU Environmental Law*, Groningen: Europa Law Publishing.

Epstein, R.A. (1973), "A Theory of Strict Liability", *Journal of Legal Studies*, 2, pp. 151-204.

Esty, D.C. & Geradin, D. (1997), "Market Access, Competitiveness and Harmonisation: Environmental Protection in Regional Trade Agreements", *Harvard Environmental Law Review*, 21, pp. 265-336.

Esty, D.C. & Geradin, D. (1998), "Environmental Protection and International Competitiveness: A Conceptual Framework", *Journal of World Trade*, 32, pp. 5-46.

Faure, M. (2003), "How Law and Economics May Contribute to the Harmonisation of Tort Law in Europe", in Zimmermann, R. (ed.), *Grundstrukturen des Europäischen Deliktsrechts*, Nomos, pp. 31-82.

Faure, M. (2012), "Effectiveness of Environmental Law: What Does the Evidence Tell Us?", *William & Mary Environmental Law and Policy Review*, 36, pp. 293-336.

Faure, M. & Fenn, P. (1999), "Retro-active Liability and the Insurability of Long-tail Risks", *International Review of Law and Economics*, 19, pp. 487-498.

Faure, M., Fernhout, F. & Philipsen, N. (2010), "No Cure, No Pay and Contingency Fees", in Tuil, M. & Visscher, L. (eds), *New Trends in Financing Civil Litigation in Europe. A Legal, Empirical, and Economic Analysis*, Cheltenham, UK and Northampton, MA: Edward Elgar, pp. 33-56.

Faure, M. & Johnston, J.S. (2009), "The Law and Economics of Environmental Federalism: Europe and the United States Compared", *Virginia Environmental Law Journal*, 27, pp. 205-274.

Faure, M. & Raja, A.V. (2010), "Effectiveness of Environmental Public Interest Litigation in India: Determining the Key Variables", *Fordham Environmental Law Review*, 21 (2), pp. 239-294.

Faure, M. & Skogh, G. (2003), *The Economic Analysis of Environmental Policy and Law: An Introduction*, Cheltenham, UK and Northampton, MA: Edward Elgar.

Fenn, P. & Rickman, N. (1999), "Delay and Settlement in Litigation", *Economic Journal*, 109, pp. 476-491.

Fenn, P. & Rickman, N. (2010), "The Empirical Analysis of Litigation Funding", in Tuil, M. & Visscher, L. (eds), *New Trends in Financing Civil Litigation*, Cheltenham, UK and Northampton, MA: Edward Elgar, pp. 131-148.

Fredriksson, P.G. & Millimet, D.L. (2002), "Strategic Interaction and the Determinants of Environmental Policy Across U.S. States", *Journal of Urban Economics*, 51, pp. 101-122.

Ginsburg, T. & Moustafa, T. (2008), *Rule by Law: The Politics of Courts in Authoritarian Regimes*, Cambridge: Cambridge University Press.

Gould, J.P. (1973), "The Economics of Legal Conflicts", *Journal of Legal Studies*, 2, pp. 279-300.

Gravelle, H. (1990), "Rationing Trials by Waiting: Welfare Implications", *International Review of Law and Economics*, 10, pp. 255-270.

Gravelle, H. (1995), "Regulating the Market for Civil Justice", in *Reform of Civil Procedure*, Oxford: Oxford University Press, pp. 279-303.

Greenstone, M. (2002), "The Impacts of Environmental Regulations on Industrial Activity: Evidence from the 1970 and 1977 Clean Air Act Amendments and the Census of Manufacturers", *Journal of Political Economy*, 110, pp. 1175-1219.

Gray, W.B. & Shadbegian, R.J. (2007), "The Environmental Performance of Polluting Plants: A Special Analysis", *Journal of Regional Science*, 47 (1), pp. 63-84.

Hay, B.L. (1995), "Effort, Information, Settlement, Trial", *Journal of Legal Studies*, 24, pp. 29-62.

Helland, E. & Klick, J. (2007), "The Effect of Judicial Expedience on Attorney Fees in Class Actions", *Journal of Legal Studies*, 36, pp. 171-187.

Iyer, V.R.K. (1994), *Declining Judicial Culture and Other Essays*, Madurai, India: Society for Community Organisation Trust.

Jaffe, A.B., Peterson, S.R., Portney, P.R. & Stavins, R.N. (1995), "Environmental Regulation and the Competitiveness of US Manufacturing: What Does the Evidence Tell Us?", *Journal of Economic Literature*, 33, pp. 132-163.

Jans, J.H. & Vedder, H.H.B. (2012), *European Environmental Law after Lisbon*, 4th edn, Groningen: Europa Law Publishing.

Jeppesen, T., List, J.A. & Folmer, H. (2002), "Environmental Regulations and New Plant Location Decisions: Evidence from a Meta-Analysis", *Journal of Regional Science*, 42, pp. 19-49.

Kaplow, L. (1986), "An Economic Analysis of Legal Transitions", *Harvard Law Review*, 99, pp. 509-617.

Katz, A. (1987), "Measuring the Demand for Litigation: Is the English Rule Really Cheaper?", *Journal of Law, Economics, and Organization,* 3, pp. 143-176.

Keske, S., Renda, A. & Van den Bergh, R. (2010), "Financing and group litigation", in Tuil, M. and Visscher, L. (eds), *New Trends in Financing Civil Litigation in Europe. A Legal, Empirical and Economic Enalysis,* Cheltenham, UK and Northampton, MA: Edward Elgar, pp. 33-56.

Kessler, D.P. & Rubinfeld, D.L. (2007), "Empirical Study of the Civil Justice System", in Polinsky, A.M. & Shavell, S. (eds), *Handbook of Law & Economics: Volume 1*, Amsterdam-Oxford: North-Holland, pp. 343-402.

Kidd, M. (2010), "Public Interest Environmental Litigation: Recent Cases Raise Possible Obstacles", *PER/PELJ*, 5 (13), pp. 26-46.

Kobayashi, B.H. & Parker, J.S. (2000), "Civil Procedure: General", in Bouckaert, B. & De Geest, G. (eds), *Encyclopedia of Law and Economics, Volume VII: Civil and Criminal Procedure*, Cheltenham, UK and Northampton, MA: Edward Elgar, pp. 1-26.

Konisky, D.M. (2008), "Regulatory Competition and Environmental Enforcement: Is There a Race to the Bottom?", *American Journal of Political Science*, 51 (4), pp. 853-872.

Landes, W.M. (1971), "An Economic Analysis of the Courts", *Journal of Law and Economics,* 14, pp. 61-107.

Landes, W.M. & Posner, R.A. (1975), "The Independent Judiciary in an Interest-Group Perspective", *Journal of Law and Economics*, 18 (3), pp. 875-901.

Levinson, A. (2003), "Environmental Regulatory Competition: A Status Report and Some New Evidence", *National Tax Journal*, 56, pp. 91-106.

List, J.A. & Gerking, S. (2000), "Regulatory Federalism and U.S. Environmental Policies", *Journal of Regional Science*, 40, pp. 453-471.

List, J.A., McHone, W.W. & Millimet, D.L. (2003), "Effects of Air Quality Regulation on the Destination Choice of Relocating Plants", *Oxford Economic Papers*, 55 (4), pp. 657-678.

List, J.A., Millimet, D.L., Fredriksson, P.G. & McHone, W.W. (2003), "Effects of Environmental Regulations on Manufacturing Plant Births: Evidence from a Propensity Score Matching Estimator", *Review of Economics and Statistics*, 85 (4), pp. 944-952.

Markusen, J., Morey, E. & Olewiler, N. (1995), "Noncooperative Equilibria in Regional Environmental Policies When Plant Locations are Endogenous", *Journal of Public Economics*, 56, pp. 55-77.

Menell, P.S. (1983), "A Note in Private Versus Social Incentives to Sue in a Costly Legal System", *Journal of Legal Studies*, 12, pp. 41-52.

Miceli, T.J. (2000), "Deterrence, Litigation Costs, and the Statute of Limitations for Tort Suits", *International Review of Law and Economics*, 20, pp. 383-394.

Milieu Ltd. (2007), *Measures on Access to Justice in Environmental Matters (Article 9(3)): Country Reports*, study for DG Environment, Brussels.

Millimet, D.L. & List, J.A. (2004), "The Case of the Missing Pollution Haven Hypothesis", *Journal of Regulatory Economics*, 26 (3), pp. 239-262.

Mühl, M. (2001), "Economic Analysis of Settlement Negotiation in a Litigation Process", *Économie Appliquée*, 3, pp. 39-74.

Mühl, M. & Vereeck, L. (2003), "Harmonization of Judicial Interest Payments and Litigation in a Federalist State", in Marciano, A. & Josselin, J.-M. (eds), *From Economic to Legal Competition*, Cheltenham, UK and Northampton, MA: Edward Elgar, pp. 121-141.

Nixon, D.C. & Haskin, J.D. (2000), "Judicial Retirement Strategies: The Judge's Role in Influencing Party Control of the Appellate Courts", *American Politics Quarterly*, 28 (4), pp. 458-489.

Oates, W.E. (1972), *Fiscal Federalism*, New York: Harcourt Brace Jovanovich.

Oates, W.E. & Schwab, R.M. (1988), "Economic Competition Among Jurisdictions: Efficiency Enhancing or Distortion Inducing?", *Journal of Public Economics*, 35, pp. 333-354.

Ogus, A.I. (1995), "Rethinking Self-Regulation", *Oxford Journal of Legal Studies*, 15 (1), pp. 97-108.

Ogus, A.I. (1999), "Competition between National Legal Systems: A Contribution of Economic Analysis to Comparative Law", *International and Comparative Law Quarterly*, 48, pp. 405-418.

Ogus, A.I. (2000), "Self-Regulation", in Bouckaert, B. & De Geest, G. (eds), *Encyclopaedia of Law and Economics,* Cheltenham, UK: Edward Elgar, vol. 9, pp. 587-602.

Olson, M. (1973), "Evaluating Performance in the Public Sector", in: Moss, M., *The Measurement of Economic and Social Performance,* NBER, New York: Columbia University Press, pp. 355-409.

P'ng, I.P.L. (1983), "Strategic Behavior in Suit, Settlement, and Trial", *Bell Journal of Economics*, 14, pp. 539-550.

Pallemaerts, M. (2009), *Compliance by the European Community with Its Obligations on Access to Justice as a Party to the Aarhus Convention*, Report for WWF-UK, Insitute for European Environmental Policy (IEEP), June 2009.

Pallemaerts, M. (2011), "Access to Environmental Justice at EU Level: Has the 'Aarhus Regulation' Improved the Situation?", in Pallemaerts, M. (ed.), *The Aarhus Convention at Ten: Interactions and Tensions between Conventional International Law and EU Environmental Law*, Groningen: Europa Law Publishing, pp. 271-312.

Philipsen, N.J. (2010), "Regulation and Competition in the Legal Profession: Developments in the EU and China", *Journal of Competition Law and Economics*, 6 (2), 2010, pp. 203-231.

Polinsky, A.M. & Rubinfeld, D.L. (1988), "The Welfare Implications of Costly Litigation for the Level of Liability", *Journal of Legal Studies*, 17, pp. 151-164.

Poncelet, C. (2012), "Access to Justice in Environmental Matters – Does the European Union Comply with its Obligations?", *Journal of Environmental Law*, 24 (2), pp. 287-309.

Posner, R.A. (1973), "An Economic Approach to Legal Procedure and Judicial Administration", *Journal of Legal Studies*, 2, pp. 399-458.

Posner, R.A. (1993), "What Do Judges and Justices Maximize? (The Same Thing Everybody Else Does)", *Supreme Court Economic Review*, 3, pp. 1-41.

Posner, R.A. (2008), *How Judges Think*, Cambridge, MA: Harvard University Press.

Posner, R.A. (2010), *Economic Analysis of Law,* 8th edn, New York: Aspen Publishers.

Pound, R. (1911), "The Scope and Purpose of Sociological Jurisprudence", *Harvard Law Review*, 25, pp. 140-168.

Priest, G.L. & Klein, B. (1984), "The Selection of Disputes for Litigation", *Journal of Legal Studies*, 13, pp. 1-55.

Pring, G. & Pring, C. (2010), *Green Injustice: Creating and Improving Environmental Courts and Tribunals: The Access Initiative*, available at: <http://tinyurl.com/7z4gnfj>.

Raiffa, H. (1968), *Decision Analysis: Introductory Lectures on Choices under Uncertainty*, Reading, MA: Addison-Wesley.

Rao, M. (2004), *Public Interest Litigation in India: A Renaissance in Social Justice,* 2nd edn, Eastern Book Co.

Rajamani, L. (2007), "Public Interest Environmental Litigation in India: Exploring Issues of Access, Participation, Equity, Effectiveness and Sustainability", *Journal of Environmental Law*, 19 (3), pp. 293-321.

Razzaque, J. (ed.) (2004), *Public Interest Environment Litigation in India, Pakistan, and Bangladesh*, special issue of the Comparative and Environment Law Series, Vol. 7, Kluwer Law International, 2004.

Revesz, R.L. (1996), "Federalism and Interstate Environmental Externalities", *University of Pennsylvania Law Review*, 144, pp. 2341-2416.

Revesz, R.L. (1992), "Rehabilitating Interstate Competition: Rethinking the Race-for-the-Bottom Rationale for Federal Environmental Regulation", *New York University Law Review*, 67, pp. 1210-1254.

Revesz, R.L. (1997a), "Federalism and Environmental Regulation: Lessons for the European Union and the International Community", *Virginia Law Review*, 83, pp. 1331-1346.

Revesz, R.L. (1997b), "The Race-to-the-Bottom and Federal Environmental Regulation: A Response to Critics", *Minnesota Law Review*, 82, pp. 535-564.

Revesz, R.L. (2000), "Federalism and Environmental Regulation: An Overview", in: Revesz, R.L., Sands, Ph. & Stewart, R.B. (eds), *Environmental Law, the Economy and Sustainable Development*, Cambridge: Cambridge University Press, pp. 37-79.

Samuelson, P. (1954), "The Pure Theory of Public Expenditures", *Review of Economics and Statistics*, 36, pp. 387-389.

Schäfer, H.B. (2000), "The Bundling of Similar Interest in Litigation. The Incentives for Class Action and Legal Actions Taken by Associations", *European Journal of Law and Economics*, 3, pp. 183-213.

Schwartz, W.F. & Tullock, G. (1975), "The Costs of a Legal System", *Journal of Legal Studies*, 4, pp. 75-82.

Seerden, R.J.G.H. (ed.) (2007), "Administrative Law of the European Union, its Member States and the United States. A Comparative Analysis", *Ius Commune Europaeum* 68, Antwerp: Intersentia, pp. 155-219.

Seerden, R.J.G.H., Heldeweg, M.A. & Deketelaere, K. (eds) (2002), *Public Environmental Law in the European Union and the United States. A Comparative Analysis*, The Hague, London, Boston: Kluwer Law International.

Shavell, S. (1982a), "Suit, Settlement and Trial: A Theoretical Analysis under Alternative Methods for the Allocation of Legal Costs", *Journal of Legal Studies*, 11, pp. 55-81.

Shavell, S. (1982b), "The Social versus the Private Incentive to Bring Suit in a Costly Legal System", *Journal of Legal Studies*, 11, pp. 333-339.

Shavell, S. (1984), "Liability for Harm versus Regulation of Safety", *Journal of Legal Studies*, 13, pp. 357-374.

Shavell, S. (1997), "The Fundamental Divergence between the Private and the Social Motive to Use the Legal System", *Journal of Legal Studies*, 26, pp. 575-613.

Shavell, S. (1999), "The Level of Litigation: Private versus Social Optimality of Suit and Settlement", *International Review of Law and Economics*, 19, pp. 99-115.

Shavell, S. (2004), *Foundations of Economic Analysis of Law*, Cambridge: Belknap Press of Harvard University Press.

Spier, K.E. (2007), "Litigation", in Polinsky, A.M. & Shavell, S. (eds), *Handbook of Law & Economics: Volume 1*, Amsterdam-Oxford: North-Holland, pp. 259-342.

Spriggs, J.F. & Wahlbeck, P.J. (1995), "Calling It Quits: Strategic Retirement on the Federal Courts of Appeals, 1893-1991", *Political Research Quarterly*, 48 (3), pp. 573-597.

Stec, S. & Casey-Lefkowitz, S. (2000), *The Aarhus Convention. An Implementation Guide*, New York and Geneva: United Nations.

Stein, L.A. (1979), "The Theoretical Basis of Locus Standi", in Stein, L.A. (ed.), *Locus Standi*, Sydney: Law Book Co.

Stras, D.R. (2006), "The Incentives Approach to Judicial Retirement", *Minnesota Law Review*, 90, pp. 1417-1446.

Tuil, M. & Visscher, L. (eds) (2010), *New Trends in Financing Civil Litigation in Europe. A Legal, Empirical, and Economic Analysis*, Cheltenham and Northampton, MA: Edward Elgar.

Tullock, G. (1980), *Trials on Trial: The Pure Theory of Legal Procedure*, New York: Columbia University Press.

Tullock, G. (1994), "Court Errors", *European Journal of Law and Economics*, 1, pp. 9-21.

Van Aaken, A. (2005), "Making International Human Rights Protection more Effective: a Rational Choice Approach to the Effectiveness of Use Standi Provisions", Max-Planck Institute for Research on Collective Goods, Preprint no. 2005-16.

Van den Bergh, R. (1994), "The Subsidiarity Principle in European Community Law: Some Insights from Law and Economics", *Maastricht Journal of European and Comparative Law*, 1, pp. 337-366.

Van den Bergh, R. (2000), "Towards an Institutional Legal Framework for Regulatory Competition in Europe", *Kyklos*, 53, pp. 435-466.

Van den Bergh, R., Faure, M. & Lefevere, J. (1996), "The Subsidiarity Principle in European Environmental Law: An Economic Analysis", in Eide, E. & Van den Bergh, R. (eds), *Law and Economics of the Environment,* Oslo: Juridisk Forlag, pp. 121-166.

Van Velthoven, B.C.J. & Van Wijck, P.W. (1997), *Recht en Efficiëntie,* Deventer: Kluwer.

Vereeck, L. & Mühl, M. (2000), "An Economic Theory of Court Delay", *European Journal of Law and Economics,* 7, pp. 243-268.

Verschuuren, J. (2005), "The Netherlands", in De Sadeleer, N., Roller, G. & Dross, M. (eds), *Access to Justice in Environmental Matters and the Role of NGOs. Empirical Findings and Legal Appraisal,* Groningen: Europa Law Publishing, pp. 97-117.

Vogel, D. (1995), *Trading up: Consumer and Environmental Regulation in a Global Economy,* Cambridge: Harvard University Press.

Vogel, D. (2004), "Trade and the Environment in the Global Economy", in Vig, N.J. & Faure, M.G. (eds), *Green Giants? Environmental Policies of the United States and the European Union,* Cambridge: MIT Press.

Wang, A. & Gao, J. (2010), "Environmental Courts and the Development of Public Interest Litigation in China", *Journal of Court Innovation,* 3 (1), pp. 37-50.

Weber, F. (2012), *Towards an Optimal Mix of Public and Private Enforcement in Consumer Law. A Comparative Law and Economics Analysis of European Consumer Law Enforcement (Package Travel vs. Misleading Advertising),* Ph.D. thesis, Erasmus School of Law, Rotterdam, 28 June 2012.

Wellisch, D. (2000), *Theory of Public Finance in a Federal State,* Cambridge: Cambridge University Press.

Wilson, J.D. (1996), "Capital Mobility and Environmental Standards: Is There a Race to the Bottom?", in Bhawati, J. & Hudec, R.P. (eds), *Fair Trade and Harmonization: Prerequisites for Free Trade,* MIT Press, pp. 393-427.

Wittman, D. (1988), "Dispute Resolution, Bargaining, and the Selection of Cases for Trial: A Study of the Generation of Biased and Unbiased Data", *Journal of Legal Studies,* 17, pp. 313-352.

Xing, Y. & Kolstad, Ch.D. (1995), "Do Lax Environmental Regulations Attract Foreign Investment?", *Environmental and Resource Economics*, 21, pp. 1-22.

Yap, P.Y. & Lau, H. (2010), *Public Interest Litigation in Asia,* New York: Routledge Law in Asia.

Zeisel, H., Kalven, H. & Buchholz, B. (1978), *Delay in the Courts,* 2nd edition, Westport: Greenwood Press.

Zhang, B. & Zhang, M. (2012), "Specialized Environment Courts in China: Status Quo, Challenges and Responses", *Journal of Energy and Natural Resources Law*, 3, pp. 2-25.

Annex 1: Questionnaire Latvia

Private litigation

• Are there any restrictions regarding private action against industries trespassing environmental law? Probably private action has to be based on the impairment of a subjective right in all cases. Should this be different?

• What is your interpretation of 9(3) Aarhus in this respect?

Definition of environmental matters

• 9(3) Aarhus does not contain or refer to a definition of "national law relating to the environment". Can this be left to the Member States or is a general applicable definition wished for?

• 9(3) Aarhus applies to "national law", which could be seen as distinct from EU directives and regulations. Could this become a problem in the future when the EU becomes more active in this field?

Suspensive effect judicial review

• Does an administrative action against an environmental decision or a judicial review action have suspensive effect?

• If so, can environmental decisions be declared provisionally enforceable by the issuing authority to prevent the suspensive effect of an action in court?

• If not, is there an effective, fast and not expensive procedure to get an interim order to obtain this suspensive effect?

• In other countries (Germany for instance), parties benefiting from administrative decisions can apply for a "go ahead"-decision in case of an action in court started by another party. Does the same apply for Latvia? If so, is this a satisfactory construction?

Outcome of the trial

• Are there any restrictions on the possible outcome of a trial in environmental matters? Could the court substitute the decision of the public authority by its own?

• Is it possible to reach the end result in a way that can be described as "adequate and effective, timely and not prohibitively expensive" in the sense of 9(4) Aarhus?

• If not, do you think the EU directive should specify that a new procedure has to be instituted that is in accordance with 9(4) Aarhus?

Consequences judiciary

• Are there statistics regarding environmental litigation in Lativia available (under whichever definition of "environmental")?

• Are there studies about the consequences of environmental litigation in the Latvian context, for instance about large projects that had to be changed substantively or repealed because of environmental litigation?
• Do you expect siginificant changes in the number of environmenal proceedings when access to justice in environmental matters would be granted to all private persons and eNGOs in all matters in which their interests (or the interests they claim to defend) are affected?

Requirements eNGOs
• 9(3) Aarhus provides that national law can set criteria for "members of the public" in order to be entitled to access to justice in environmental matters. This can be translated into requirements for NGOs, like being an eNGO, existing for a certain number of years, statutory objectives and actual activities. Should these criteria better be left to the Member States?
• When the EU decides to impose restrictions on these criteria, which restrictions would be acceptable in your view? Is recognition by a public authority (as is nowadays the case in Germany) necessary in your view?
• Would litigation significantly increase when ad hoc-eNGOs (established to litigate in one specific case, for instance the construction of a new highway) would have to be allowed to commence proceedings?
• Is transborder litigation by eNGOs acceptable according to "the Latvian view" on litigation in environmental matters?

Actio popularis and class action
• Did the introduction of an *actio popularis* in environmental matters in Lativia have significant consequences for litigation and the judiciary in general? Are there statistics available, comparing the old situation with the new?
• Should class action be allowed in environmental matters? How do you estimate the effects of the introduction of class actions in Latvian procedural law?

Third party protection
• In private and administrative litigation two parties are opposing each other, whereas the interests of third parties are directly concerned. Is there a possibility for the third party to join the proceedings in order to be heard? Do you see a task for the EU in this respect?

Measures to obviate frivolous claims
• Extending access to justice will always increase the risk of more frivolous or unmeritorious claims. Which measures have been taken in Latvia to prevent against these claims?

To what extent have these measures been effective? Do you think the Latvian approach needs to be changed?

Litigation costs

- Are there any measures in force to prevent against litigation costs that would keep parties from commencing proceedings? Do you think they are effective?
- In what way expert costs are divided over the parties and the State? Is this in accordance with the principle of access to justice in environmental matters?
- Is public interest litigation (PIL) facilitated in your country? Would an enhancement of PIL help courts with the enforcement of environmental law?
- Have there been any studies in your country regarding the influence of costs on litigation in environmental matters?

Leveling the playing field

- Do you have any experience with disparity of applying of EU environmental rules in different countries affecting the position of Latvian industry? Do you have reasons to believe that Latvian industry would welcome the idea of a uniform access to justice in environmental matters in all EU Member States?

Mediation

- Could mediation be a reasonable alternative to litigation in environmental matters in the Latvian context? Would this be a two- or a three-party-mediation?

Annex 2: Questionnaire UK

Private litigation

- Are there any restrictions regarding private action against industries trespassing environmental law? Probably private action has to be based on the impairment of a subjective right in all cases. Should this be different?
- What is your interpretation of 9(3) Aarhus in this respect?

Definition of environmental matters

- 9(3) Aarhus does not contain or refer to a definition of "national law relating to the environment". Can this be left to the Member States or is a general applicable definition wished for?
- 9(3) Aarhus applies to "national law", which could be seen as distinct from EU directives and regulations. Could this become a problem in the future when the EU becomes more active in this field?

Suspensive effect judicial review

- Does a judicial review action have suspensive effect?
- If so, can environmental decisions be declared provisionally enforceable by the issuing authority to prevent the suspensive effect of a judicial review action?
- If not, is there an effective, fast and not expensive procedure to get an interim order to obtain this suspensive effect?
- In other countries (Germany for instance), parties benefiting from administrative decisions can apply for a "go ahead"-decision in case of judicial review started by another party. Does the same apply for the UK? If so, is this a satisfactory construction?

Outcome of the trial

- Are there any restrictions on the possible outcome of judicial review of environmental decisions of public authorities? Could the court substitute the decision of the public authority by its own?
- Is it possible to reach the end result in a way that can be described as "adequate and effective, timely and not prohibitively expensive" in the sense of 9(4) Aarhus?
- If not, do you think the EU directive should specify that a new procedure has to be instituted that is in accordance with 9(4) Aarhus?

Consequences judiciary

- Are there statistics regarding environmental litigation in the UK available (under whichever definition of "environmental")?

• Are there studies about the consequences of environmental litigation in the UK context, for instance about large projects that had to be changed substantively or repealed because of environmental litigation?
• Do you expect siginificant changes in the number of environmenal proceedings when access to justice in environmental matters would be granted to all private persons and eNGOs in all matters in which their interests (or the interests they claim to defend) are affected?

Requirements eNGOs
• 9(3) Aarhus provides that national law can set criteria for "members of the public" in order to be entitled to access to justice in environmental matters. This can be translated into requirements for NGOs, like being an eNGO, existing for a certain number of years, statutory objectives and actual activities. Should these criteria better be left to the Member States?
• When the EU decides to impose restrictions on these criteria, which restrictions would be acceptable in your view? Is recognition by a public authority (as is nowadays the case in Germany) necessary in your view?
• Would litigation significantly increase when adhoc-eNGOs (established to litigate in one specific case, for instance the construction of a new highway) would have to be allowed to commence proceedings?
• Is transborder litigation by eNGOs acceptable according to "the UK view" on litigation in environmental matters?

Actio popularis and class action
• Would the introduction of an *actio popularis* in environmental matters have significant consequences for litigation and the judiciary in general?
• Should class action be allowed in environmental matters? How do you estimate the effects of the introduction of class actions in UK procedural law?

Third party protection
• In private and administrative litigation two parties are opposing each other, whereas the interests of third parties are directly concerned. Is there a possibility for the third party to join the proceedings in order to be heard? Do you see a task for the EU in this respect?

Measures to obviate frivolous claims
• Extending access to justice will always increase the risk of more frivolous or unmeritorious claims. Which measures in your view are acceptable or necessary to prevent against these claims?

Litigation costs

- Are there any measures in force to prevent against litigation costs that would keep parties from commencing proceedings? Do you think they are effective?
- In what way expert costs are divided over the parties and the State? Is this in accordance with the principle of access to justice in environmental matters?
- Is Public Interest Litigation (PIL) facilitated in your country? Would an enhancement of PIL help courts with the enforcement of environmental law?
- Have there been any studies in your country regarding the influence of costs on litigation in environmental matters?

Leveling the playing field

- Do you have any experience with disparity of applying of EU environmental rules in different countries affecting the position of UK industry? Do you have reasons to believe that UK industry would welcome the idea of a uniform access to justice in environmental matters in all EU Member States?

Mediation

- Could mediation be a reasonable alternative to litigation in environmental matters in the UK context? Would this be a two- or a three-party-mediation?

Annex 3: Questionnaire Germany

Private litigation

• Are there any restrictions regarding private action against industries that violate environmental law? Probably in Germany private action has to be based on the impairment of a subjective right in all cases. Should this according to you be different?

• What is your interpretation of Article 9(3) Aarhus in this respect?

Definition of environmental matters

• Article 9(3) Aarhus does not include a definition of "national law relating to the environment". Can this be left to the Member States indeed or is a general applicable definition wished for?

• Article 9(3) Aarhus applies to "national law", which could be seen as distinct from EU Directives and Regulations. Could this become a problem in the future when the EU becomes more active in this field?

Suspensive effect administrative action

• Environmental decisions can be declared provisionally enforceable by the issuing authority to prevent the suspensive effect of an administrative action. Is this declaration standard? Shouldn't this be a matter for the courts? Is an EU-imposed system desirable?

• Parties benefiting from administrative decisions can apply for a "go ahead"-decision in case of judicial review started by another party. Is this a satisfactory construction?

Outcome of the trial

• The possible outcome of the trial depends on the type of action (*Anfechtungsklage*, *Verpflichtungsklage/Leistungsklage*, *Feststellungsklage*). Do you see a conflict with Article 9(4) Aarhus, that requires "adequate and effective" remedies? Could you assess the consequences when the type of outcome would be general for all environmental cases?

Consequences judiciary

• Are there statistics regarding environmental litigation available in Germany?

• Are there studies about the consequences of environmental litigation in the German context, for instance about large projects that had to be changed substantively or repealed because of environmental litigation?

• Do you expect siginificant changes in the number of environmental proceedings when access to justice in environmental matters would be granted to all private persons and eNGOs in all matters in which their interests (or the interests they claim to defend) are affected?

Requirements eNGOs

• 9(3) Aarhus provides that national law can set criteria for "members of the public" in order to be entitled to access to justice in environmental matters. This can be translated into requirements for NGOs, like being an eNGO, existing for a certain number of years, statutory objectives and actual activities. Should these criteria better be left to the Member States?

• When the EU decides to impose restrictions on these criteria, which restrictions would be acceptable in your view? Is recognition (as is nowadays the case in Germany) necessary in your view?

• Would litigation significantly increase when *ad hoc* eNGOs (established to litigate in one specific case, for instance the construction of a new highway) would have to be allowed to commence proceedings?

• Is transborder litigation by eNGOs acceptable according to "the German view" on litigation in environmental matters?

Actio popularis and class action

• Would the introduction of an *actio popularis* in environmental matters have significant consequences for litigation and the judiciary in general?

• Should class action be allowed in environmental matters? How do you estimate the effects of the introduction of class actions in German procedural law?

Third party protection

• In private and administrative litigation, parties are opposed, whereas the interests of third parties are directly concerned. In German procedural law, this can be overcome by the "*Beiladung*". Do you see a task for the EU in this respect?

Measures to obviate frivolous claims

• Extending access to justice will always increase the risk of more frivolous claims. Which measures in your view are acceptable or necessary to prevent against these claims?

Litigation costs

• Are there any measures in forces to prevent against litigation costs that would keep parties from commencing proceedings? Do you think they are effective?

• In what way expert costs are divided over the parties and the State? Is this in accordance with the principle of access to justice in environmental matters?

• Is public interest litigation (PIL) facilitated in Germany? Would an enhancement of PIL help courts with the enforcement of environmental law?

• Have there been any studies in your country regarding the influence of costs on litigation in environmental matters?

Leveling the playing field

- Do you have reasons to believe that German industry would welcome the idea of a uniform access to justice in environmental matters in all EU Member States? For example, because a harmonised system may lead to a "level playing field" for industry.

Mediation

- Does or should mediation play a role in Germany?